A Battered Proud Badge

Tales of Policing a Young Country

A Battered Proud Badge

Tales of Policing a Young Country.

Robert Rattenbury

Rangitawa
PUBLISHING

A Battered Proud Badge - Tales of Policing a Young Country
Published by Rangitawa Publishing, Feilding, New Zealand. 2020.

ISBN 978-09951406-3-9

www.rangitawapublishing.com
rangitawa@xtra.co.nz

With Thanks to:-

Sherwood Young MA (Hons), MBE, Chief Inspector (Retired)
Glenn Dixon LLB (Hons), Detective (Retired)
Murray Horn, Constable (Retired)
Detective 1 (Retired) and Senior Constable 2 (Retired) – Special thanks for your courage.
Tony Smith, Senior Sergeant (Retired.)
Rowan Carroll, MA, PGDMS, BEd, Curator New Zealand Police Museum.
Caroline Barron, LoveWordsMusic. www.carolinebarronauthor.com
Jill Darragh, Rangitawa Publishing

Dedicated to:-

All serving and no longer serving women and men of the New Zealand Police
Especially my own "blue" family
William (Bill) Knox (RIP), Constable (Resigned) – Uncle
Kevin Knox, Senior Sergeant (Retired) - Cousin
Sarahlee Rattenbury, Non-sworn, (Resigned) – Sister
Senior Constable Luke Rattenbury – Serving - Son
And especially the women in my life
Jenny, Jodie, Charlotte, McKenna and Maisie

"We sleep safe in our beds because rough men (and women) stand ready in the night to visit violence on those who would do us harm."

George Orwell - supposedly

*"I, **Robert David Rattenbury** do swear that I will well and truly serve our Sovereign Lady the Queen in the Police, without favour or affection, malice or ill-will, until I am legally discharged; that I will see and cause Her Majesty's peace to be kept and preserved; that I will prevent to the best of my power all offences against the peace; and that while I continue to hold the said office I will to the best of my skill and knowledge discharge all the duties thereof faithfully according to law. So help me God."*

<u>Oath taken at time of attestation of Constable RD Rattenbury 6800P on 24th August 1971</u>

Foreword

As a recently retired member of the Police and having had a long-standing interest in history generally; I was pleased to be asked to review Rob Rattenbury's latest book, "A Battered but Proud Badge".

This book is an eclectic mix of stories which range from the beginnings of the NZ Police from the Armed Constabulary in 1886; through the political machinations of the government of the time and the Police Commissioner Cullen in their dealing with Rua Kenana, of the Tuhoe tribe in the Uruweras in 1916; the sinking of the Wahine in 1968 and the subsequent police response.

He also recounts in detail various notable murders and incidents that accelerated change in the New Zealand Police with tactics and administration.

The detailed account of the search, arrest and subsequent trial of Pawelka for the alleged murder of a policeman, Sergeant John MacGuire in Palmerston North in 1910 is well set out and reflects the high level of concern felt by the public and media at that time during the manhunt for Pawelka; as can be seen from the media accounts of that time, questioning the police management and tactics.

The story of the hunt for Stanley Graham near Hokitika on the West Coast in October 1941, and the subsequent shooting of seven people, five being Police officers, further cements his view of the negative impact upon police attitudes and tactical responses in a somewhat negative way for the next two decades.

Rob's writing is extremely effective in setting out the employment and social conditions of the day in New Zealand from the period 1880s until the beginning of the first World War. He paints a picture of how men from extremely rough backgrounds, often with previous criminal convictions were able to join the police. These men came from all parts of the world, gold fields, logging camps and very hard physical rural jobs. Often uneducated and violent, they were working for an organisation that was very inflexible and severe in their staff management practices.

Rob's relaxed style of writing takes you into the incident and is very effective in making you feel that you are present and witnessing what took place, which is something often missing from historical narratives and makes this book easy to read and both entertaining and informative.

He details various incidents of murders attended by the police and police officers being shot in the period 1941 until the early 1960s which highlight the mindset of the Police administration and staff as to how such incidents should be attended and what role firearms took when attending.

This mind-set or attitude came to an end in 1963 because of two major shootings in three months where four police officers and one civilian were shot in January and four weeks later in February 1963.

The shootings of Detective Inspector Wallace Chalmers and Detective Sergeant Neville Power in the Waitakarere Ranges in January followed four weeks later by Constable Jim Richardson and Bryan Schultz in Lower Hutt attending a domestic incident were lightning rods for change in police attitudes and tactics.

Rob's detailed account explains why this led to the introduction of specialised training for attending armed incidents utilising the newly created Armed Offender Squads (AOS) through-out the country.

The book also highlights the somewhat nefarious relationship between the Police, publicans, bookmakers, prostitutes and criminals and the difficulties this caused for supervisors in maintaining the delicate balance between obtaining information and retaining the confidence of the community.

Social commentary regarding the police role in the Rua Kenana arrest in 1916 is still relevant today with Police still having to keep the peace between various groups involved in protests, sit-ins and occupation of disputed land ownership in Maori land issues and Treaty settlements.

I thoroughly recommend this book, as Rob's relaxed style of writing takes you into the incidents and is very effective in making you feel that you are present and witnessing what took place, which is something often missing from historical narratives and makes this book both easy to read and both entertaining and informative.

Tony Smith
Senior Sergeant of Police (Retired)

Contents

Introduction

My first book, So You Want To Be A Cop, was a memoir of growing up in New Zealand and tales from my time as a member of the New Zealand Police. I also traversed my family history in this country.

This book is still about policing but goes back to the formation of the police in New Zealand, touching on the first police to arrive in 1840 but mainly from the late 1860s, transforming into the New Zealand Police as we know it today. The development of New Zealand's police services over the last 180 odd years is virtually a mirror of the development of European settlement in New Zealand. Where New Zealand frontier European society went the police service of the time would come along, dragging its feet a bit, but slowly developing into the modern service New Zealand enjoys today.

You will read about bad police, good police, interesting Commissioners, a Commissioner, John "Bruce" Young, who helped to start the first New Zealand police union, the New Zealand Police Association, in the mid-thirties after being involved in an aborted attempt just before World War 1, this being stopped by the then Commissioner John Cullen. Young went on to become Commissioner, a greater achievement than would be normal with his union-focused background, just in time to deal with the 1951 Waterfront Lockout, becoming ill and passing away a short time later. He was a visionary for his time who inherited what some say was a broken, war-weary and, perhaps slightly dodgy police service but never had the chance to change it despite bringing in some enlightened views and equipment.

You will read about his successor, Commissioner Eric

Compton, whose reign was short and very eventful, resulting in the appointment of a civilian controller-General for some years, only the third time in the history of policing in New Zealand for this to happen.

The tales are based on history texts completed by several qualified and highly respected historians in the late 20th century as well as stories from books published by individual police districts as part of the 1986 centenary of the founding of the New Zealand Police. The history of our police is not all sweetness and light.

There are tales of evil, criminal police and tales of tragedy. New Zealand has been lucky to have a largely corrupt-free police service however there has been times when this has not always been the case, resulting in several Commissions of Inquiry over the past 140 years. Incompetence through lack of education, training, poor selection of recruits and bad leadership and management practices comes through in many of these stories as well.

I include a chapter about police being involved in the Intelligence and Spy game from about the start of World War 2 until the formation of the Security intelligence Service. I believe the police are better out of the security services although I am sure they can nowadays technically and professionally foot it with any intelligence service in the western world.

I believe all police services, no matter where, go through periods of great challenge and change, usually resulting in an improved service for a period of time until the next crisis arises.

When reading the old stories in this book remember to keep them in the context of the times they occurred. New Zealand was, up until the mid-20th century, a fairly rough and ready place to live and being a cop back then was very different to what you would expect today. Crooked cops were never put up with but very occasionally they managed to hang around a bit longer than they should have or to be allowed to leave with some baubles of office intact for political or, perhaps, emotional reasons.

You will read about the police never being allowed to strike or form "combinations" to request better working conditions, resulting in the formation in 1936 of the New Zealand Police Association or the police union.

A police strike in New Zealand at Russell in 1840 was likely the first industrial strike of any sort in New Zealand's history with a police boat crew going on strike for better conditions and pay, failing miserably being dismissed forthwith and receiving one month's imprisonment for their troubles, also among the first prisoners in the young soon-to-be colony.

The tales from yesteryear end with the Wahine tragedy in1968. At that time probably the biggest police rescue operation conducted in New Zealand history. 1968 is a timely year to end the old stories, being two years before I joined the police as a cadet. Part of the story of the Wahine disaster is a poem composed by a school-mate and life-long friend of mine, Terry Jordan, as a memory of Wahine Day through the eyes of a school-boy finding himself at a closed school, away from home that day.

The exception to this time-line is the stories of two Constables involved in tragic shootings in the late 20th century. Events that were tragic for the families of the deceased and somewhat traumatic for the Constables.

Today's modern New Zealand Police is a very diverse group in terms of ethnicity, gender and sexual orientation compared to the service I joined in 1970. Women, Maori and Pacifica were present in small numbers then compared to today's enlightened times, sexual orientation different from heterosexuality was obviously present but certainly not acknowledged or accepted in any shape or form. Homosexual men in the police, if outed, would lose their careers and could, theoretically, up until 1985, lose their freedom as well. "Muzza", an experienced and tough street cop, describes what life was like as a gay cop in the 1970s. A sobering tale of a good cop trying to live two lives. I am sure Muzza was not alone with his secret life back then. Different times.

New Zealand's police was, for the period from about 1880 to 1920, male and white with the exception of several non-permanent part-time Maori District and Native Constables and several matrons. William Carran broke the glass ceiling for Maori in 1920, rising to Assistant Commissioner. His is an interesting story.

New Zealand was probably about the last of the white British Empire countries to swear women in as Constables during World War 2 despite attempts by various individuals and lobby groups dating back to the start of World War 1 to make this happen. The leadership of the Police was mostly a hide-bound, conservative and unimaginative lot with a brilliant few exceptions, no-one wanting to rock the boat in what was generally a very British and conservative society.

The story of New Zealand's women police is summarised, starting with possibly the first female detective employed world-wide in 1892, Ursula Smith, the introduction of four community-based Assistant Matrons in 1917 and then the swearing in of 10 plain clothed female Constables in 1941 and leading to the situation today where at the end of April 2016 women comprised 18.9 percent (1669) of 8831 constabulary staff and 32.7 percent of recruits. Under the 2016 four-year plan, the target was for women to be 21-24 percent of constabulary staff and 50 percent of recruits by 30 June 2019. At the time of writing these were the latest figures available. Sworn police number around 10,000 in New Zealand.

I have also written some further observations on my time in the police, some of the quirkier sides of policing back in the late 20th century. Policing today is, from what I am told, a very different kettle of fish. I am not sure cops like I used to be would fit in easily in today's modern police. We were good honest people, well-educated for our time, physically very fit and tough but society accepted more in some ways from us than it would put up with today from its police.

Like any longer serving retired cop I have many stories but there are also many that can never be written down. Some are simply too distasteful for various reasons, the participants or their families may be still alive. Some are too sensitive in terms of operational or legal matters to air here. Some are, whilst interesting, inconsequential to a wider audience. Most of these stories are well-known by many past and serving police in New Zealand today but I leave them for someone to write about in the years to come.

I am a story-teller, not an historian. Please forgive any errors of fact you may find, missed by me. This is not a research paper, just, I hope, a bundle of interesting yarns really.

.

Looking Back 180 Years

Murderous Police

"When a member of the Police commits a crime it is essentially a twofold offence – for not only does he offend against the criminal code, but he breaches the trust inherent in his position. He also undermines the public confidence in the organisation that works so hard to protect its integrity and credibility. What is often overlooked is the fact that: the offender's crime is investigated, the evidence gathered and presented, and the offender is himself arrested – by policemen. So jealously do police guard their reputation that when one of their number commits a crime it is investigated and prosecuted with even greater zeal and care than if the offender was a member of the public." – Ref C R O'Hara, Northland Made to Order p.72.

A sad fact of life is that there have been police who have let evil rule them in New Zealand. Here are three cases from the annals of history that sadly show that serving police are not above committing the ultimate crime, the taking of another's life with criminal intent. The first case quoted resulted in the offending Constable being sentenced to death but history is quiet on whether or not he hung. He does not feature in Sherwood Young's record of hangings in his book Guilty on The Gallows.

The second case is clearly very suspicious but the suspect continued to serve for some years however the most recent case quoted ended in imprisonment for the offender.

On 20th March 1871 Sergeant James Collins of the Armed Constabulary stationed at Rangiaowhia, heard a shot fired near the blockhouse and a man call out that he was shot. Upon entering the blockhouse Collins found Constable J B Gilfillan lying on the floor with fellow Constables Schofield and Beattie alongside him. Gilfillan was tended to and a doctor summonsed as well as Sub-Inspector Smith from nearby Kihikihi. It was reported that Constable Thomas Pollock Muirhead had shot Gilfillan. Collins asked Gilfillan what cause he had given Muirhead to shoot him and Gilfillan, in great pain and dying, replied that Muirhead had just come into the room, levelled his rifle at him and shot him. Gilfillan died later that day from a bullet wound to the left breast.

Sergeant George Skene gave evidence that he heard a shot and saw Muirhead come out of the blockhouse with his rifle in his hand saying "Ah, a traitor can't live. Look at all those Maoris in front". Skene took the rifle from Muirhead and detained him. There was no history whatsoever of discord between Muirhead and the victim. Muirhead provided no explanation for his behavior and was tried in Auckland for murder, convicted and sentenced to death despite a jury recommendation for mercy.

This was in the last few years of the Armed Constabulary and it must be remembered that the men were mostly a rough and ready lot, many being ex-military or Irish Constabulary. Many were not trained police but ex-soldiers, despite holding police ranks. This is not the only tale of fatal outcomes of disputes between Constables. Drink and isolation played a big part in the discipline issues of the Armed Constabulary. In 1871 the New Zealand Wars were in their dying days so life was reasonably cheap on the front lines.

In the later years of the 19th century the New Zealand Police was going through a rough patch, resulting in a Commission of Inquiry in 1898 and the subsequent "weeding out" of old, inefficient and perhaps corrupt NCOs in the following years leading up to another inquiry in 1905. One NCO to escape close scrutiny for his behavior was Sergeant William Ramsay. He had joined the police in its founding year, 1886 and despite a serious incident in 1897 and possibly compromising and perjuring himself on behalf of another member in the 1898 Commission as a constable survived to be later promoted to sergeant.

The serious incident in 1897 surrounded the death of 19 year old William Lindegreen. Ramsay, who was stationed at Wairoa as the local constable, was drinking with a group of his friends who were farewelling Lindegreen from the town for some reason. The following morning the youth, an excellent swimmer, was found dead in the Wairoa River. Ramsay "investigated" the death and stated that the drowning had been suicide as Lindegreen had been embezzling money from his employer and this was about to be found out. History is silent on this point.

Rumours in the village had it that Ramsay and Lindegreen were both vying for the attentions of the local vicar's daughter Euphemia Cato, these rumours backed by inquiries made by the local press. An inquiry was demanded by Lindegreen's family as Ramsay had not advised that, at the previous night's drinks, he and Lindegreen had gone rowing in the river afterwards and that Ramsay had been drunk. A Napier detective began investigating the case and Ramsay was summarily transferred from Wairoa on the grounds that he was "clearly becoming too familiar with a certain class". The inquiry stuttered to a halt until "new evidence" in 1899 saw abortive attempts to start another inquiry. By this time Ramsay was a sergeant in Auckland. In 1906 Lindegreen's mother repeated her claim that her son had been murdered by Ramsay and the detective based in Napier who had conducted the initial homicide inquiry, did not refute this claim when asked. Ramsay still stayed until he was sacked in 1911, after 25 years' service, for being absent from duty and falsely claiming to have visited his constables on the beat during that time.

The third case revolved around a debt incurred by Constable H Barrett, stationed at Mangonui Police station in 1942. Barrett had borrowed 250 pounds from a 38 year old local gum-digger Mate Urlich, who received a promissory note given in return. Barrett and Urlich had been on good terms for some years.

On Monday, 20th July 1942 Barrett approached Urlich at his camp near Lake Ohaia and told him that the American military, then stationed in New Zealand, were interested in building an airfield near his shack. After a cup of tea they walked about a mile to inspect the site, Barrett drawing a plan in his notebook. While walking through scrub in single file Urlich heard two shots, felt a stinging pain and swung around to see Barrett, a couple of yards behind, dropping a revolver. Urlich prevented the Constable from picking it up and Barrett ran away, falling into a nearby gum hole. Urlich sought help at a local farm house and was admitted to Mangonui Hospital where the doctor removed one of his kidneys. Following the operation Urlich made a remarkable recovery, despite the fact that both bullets were still lodged in his body.

An inquiry was begun by Inspector J Fox of Whangarei with help from the Detective Branch and Barrett subsequently made a full confession to the shooting. He later pleaded guilty to attempted murder and at the Supreme Court sentencing the presiding Justice said "It was a cold blooded attempt to avoid payment that the prisoner set out to take a man's life. It was only by skilful medical attention that his life had been saved and the prisoner had avoided a charge of murder". Barrett got 7 years imprisonment with hard labour. Barrett was highly regarded by his local community, a hard working member of the local school committee and highly thought of by colleagues and supervisors. His actions were regarded as highly uncharacteristic.

Mate Urlich then sought compensation for his injuries, no ACC in those days, and after three attempts, in May 1952, almost ten years after the shooting, he was awarded 1,000 pounds by the government. I am not sure if Barrett repaid the 250 pound debt, I suspect not.

I know of two more homicides committed by serving police, both domestic related but too raw to talk of here. I guess there have been others over the years.

Unsolved Police Murder – Constable James Dorgan

Since the formation of the New Zealand Police in 1886 30 members of Police have been slain in the course of their duties with many others dying by accident or illness acquired through their duties.

Of the 30 police homicides all but one have been solved and a suspect identified. One accused, Joseph Pawelka, was acquitted of murder of Sergeant John McGuire on 9 April 1910 in Palmerston North, that murder remaining unresolved to this day.

Some of the offenders died by their own hand or were shot by Police at the time and several committed to care due to mental health issues.

However there is one police killing that is still a cold case, the shooting death of Constable James Dorgan in Timaru in the early hours of 27th August 1921 whilst he was attending a "burglars on" incident at the local clothing store T&J Thompson Drapers.

James was born in County Kerry, Ireland on 26 January 1884, migrating to New Zealand with his parents and two brothers when a teenager. After leaving school and working in a variety of jobs in Christchurch, where his family settled, he, like many young Irish men, joined the New Zealand Police and was appointed Constable 1764 at Christchurch on 11 July 1912 at the age of 28. He was described as a big man, a friendly and easy-going cop who did his job well and was much respected by his colleagues in both Christchurch and later Timaru where he transferred on 29 March 1915 to marry his sweetheart Minnie Shine.

James and Minnie set up home in rental accommodation in Timaru and soon had their first child. Minnie suffered poor health and pregnancy exacerbated her problems. Due to wanting to look after his ill wife and young baby James applied for a transfer to Temuka, a country station, where he would be able to spend more time with his family and tend to his sick wife. The application was declined, a single man getting the job instead. In those days the Police liked single men as they could be transferred at a moment's notice and did not have the worries of housing that a family man had. They lived as lodgers or in barracks.

Money was very short for James and Minnie, a Constable earning, in those days, less than a normal working man. A second child arrived in 1917 and then a third in 1919. Prior to the third birth James applied for a transfer to Waimate, another small station where he would be able to live a more settled lifestyle, enabling him to look after his wife and family better.

James could not find affordable rental accommodation in Timaru as most vacant house were left empty by owners rather than rent them out due to the hassle of having tenants. That sounds familiar 100 years later. This application was declined and James wrote to the then Commissioner asking for reconsideration. This was declined. They had to move three times in as many months due to owners wanting to sell their homes and not allowing further tenancy.

In the meantime James carried on his duties in an efficient and proper way, earning and maintaining the respect of his colleagues and fellow citizens until the evening of 26/27th August 1921. At 9.00 p.m. James and his two shift mates, Constables Thomas Christopher and McCullough, began their night shift beats, James and Christopher working the two beats, each alone, in the main street of Timaru, Stafford Street and McCullough working number 3 beat which took in the back streets of the town centre.

Christopher walked past Thompson's at about 12.40 a.m.

and saw a flash of light in the building. He watched from the darkened street but saw no further flashes. He then signaled to James, further up the street, with his torch, James arriving shortly after. While both officers checked the building again, finding it secure, they saw another flash from within the building. James told Christopher to get Thompson, the keyholder, so they could open the shop. Christopher took off and James walked down a side alley to the rear of the property to keep watch in the dark.

Christopher roused Thompson and then ran back to the shop, passing three bystanders. At this point they all heard four shots. Christopher went to the alleyway and by the light of the moon he saw a figure staggering towards him. It was James, who upon seeing his friend cried "Christopher, I am done". He fell to the ground taking Christopher, who was trying to hold him, down too. Christopher asked where the offender was but James said that he had fired four shots and went up the back, a bank at the rear of the yard. The three bystanders tried to help Christopher and he sent two to get help from other off duty police staff and a doctor. Shortly after Dr Ussher arrived James passed, death recorded at 1.30 a.m. He was the the fifth New Zealand Police member to be murdered on duty since 1886.

A major inquiry started under Senior Detective Allan Cameron and Detective James Bickerdike of Christchurch, both very experienced and hard-nosed investigators.

The enquiry found two fingerprints at the scene which could not be eliminated after a long exercise of printing any and everyone who had been in the shop. Several young men were, at various times, suspects but one-by-one were ticked off the list due to alibis and other enquiries. From reading Scott Bainbridge's very good account in his book on New Zealand cold case murders, Shot in the Dark, the homicide enquiry was extremely thorough and meticulous in detail but eventually came up short. Not the result the then

Commissioner O'Donovan, was happy with, nor the good people of Timaru.

Of note, prior to James dying he said when asked by McCullough what happened "I was shot Mac. I don't know who it is and he got me in the backyard". All the suspects identified in the enquiry, local lads, were known personally by James through his prior dealings with them or their families. The scene examination also showed that the offender was not used to the area and the points of egress and exit to the back yard, leading the team to consider that the crime was committed by an out-of-towner, possibly two.

Some scuttlebutt has arisen over the years since this murder, implicating some Police in Timaru at the time in a commercial burglary ring and also the opinion that James was shot by a serving member of police. Nothing in my reading of all the texts and books about this murder supports this theory. I have not read the investigation file but Scott Bainbridge tells me he has and this is quiet on any such theory. What is of interest is that all serving police had to provide alibis at the time to the investigation team so there must have been some theory afoot here at some stage in the inquiry.

The great grand-daughter of James told Scott Bainbridge that it was a long held family belief that Thomas Christopher murdered James. The sequence of events, timings and other people present with Christopher when the shots were heard discounts this story. Also Christopher and James were friends, of similar service, and had worked together for some years. No doubt James would have named him when asked by McCullough after he was shot.

However, as an interesting aside, Christopher left the Police later in 1921, upset that it could have been him who had been shot if James had left him and gone for help. In May 1925 a draper in Greymouth reported to Police that he suspected one of his employees of stealing rolls of sheeting and off-loading it to his competitors or selling it on the black market.

An undercover operation was begun by Detective (later Commissioner) JB Young, the grandfather of our very well-known authority on Police history in New Zealand, Sherwood Young. He caught Thomas Christopher red-handed passing four dozen pairs of towels to a member of a rival drapery firm. A subsequent search of Christopher's lodgings found further stolen property and a .45 cal. Webley revolver which he admitted to owning when in the police in Timaru. James was shot with a .32 cal. bullet, probably from a S&W revolver.

On hearing of the arrest the then Commissioner ordered that the Dorgan homicide be re-opened with a view to having Christopher charged with the murder of James. This was quickly put right with the statements taken at the time of the murder from the three bystanders with Christopher when the shots were heard from the direction of the store.

Interesting about Christopher's subsequent involvement in thefts of drapery!!

James's wife Minnie was left with three young children to struggle on with a small police pension. The country rallied to her cause and a fund formed to raise money for the family. No MSD in those days folks.

A very sad story.

Manhunt ends in double tragedy – Joseph Pawelka

The story on one of New Zealand's most infamous and ultimately successful prison escapers, Joseph Pawelka, and the antics of the Police and good citizenry of Palmerston North in early April 1910 makes for interesting but sad reading.

The manhunt supposedly run by the Police but also comprised of groups of armed vigilantes would see two innocent men killed, both in disputed circumstances.

Pawelka was a well-known and successful burglar living in the Palmerston North area in 1910. He was arrested by Detective Thomas Quirke and a Constable in February of that year for "housebreaking, entering and theft" and was remanded in custody at the Palmerston North Police Gaol. He escaped by climbing the yard walls. This led to his being branded a "very dangerous criminal". He was, shortly afterwards, recaptured and sent to the lock up at Wellington Lambton Quay police station where he again escaped on 23 March.

He subsequently made his way back to the Manawatu and he began to get the blame for a string of offending in the district, including a highway robbery near Foxton on 2 April. Two fires in Palmerston North were laid at his feet as arson, Palmerston North High School and a local furniture shop were destroyed in separate incidents on 5 April. The press were fanning the "state of great excitement" in the town and district by using such sensationalist headlines as "Manawatu's Mad Fortnight".

By then New Zealand's biggest manhunt was underway. Local businessmen took to sleeping at their premises with firearms at the ready. Two mounted Constables shot at a man near Pahiatua who they suspected was Pawelka. Armed citizen vigilante groups flourished in the town and district. Commentators from outside the district criticised these actions but the local police welcomed citizen support. Police National Headquarters also treated the manhunt very seriously, and before long there were 60 police and authorised personnel searching for Pawelka with many more unofficial volunteers, all armed. Pawelka attempted to reconcile with his estranged wife at Ashhurst but escaped when she raised the alarm. There was talk of calling out the Territorials and even drafting in regular soldiers.

On 10 April police were advised that Pawelka was attempting a burglary at his former employer's house. The house was surrounded and a decision was made to rush it. An unarmed Sergeant John McGuire, who had just transferred to Palmerston North 48 hours previously with his wife and family, ran across the front lawn and grappled with a figure he saw in the doorway to the house. Detective A Quartermain and the owner of the property, Mr Hampton, rushed around from the back. Quartermain was armed. In the dark shots rang out and McGuire fell with a stomach wound. The intruder escaped in the confusion. McGuire was in a bad way and died on 14 April. He was able to be interviewed prior to his passing and, when questioned as to why he did not have a firearm that night, replied "I am glad I didn't, I would not have used it at any rate, I might have shot him, but I am better pleased that he shot me." When asked who had shot him McGuire said that he did not think it was Detective Quartermain but it might have been.

At this time the New Zealand Police was going through a very quiet period and the population was encouraged to "self-police" with the police adopting a "softly softly" approach to their work, resulting in what some observers stated was an unwillingness and an inability of the Police to deal with serious incidents. Police were being criticised for being too kind and gentle. A new police maxim that came about after this tragedy was "Don't do a McGuire", in other words, don't be too easy going and benign.

The "quiet, unassuming" McGuire was a former grocer who had spent 14 years on police clerical work before his transfer to Palmerston North less than 48 hours before the shooting. He sought the transfer as he thought the outside work would benefit his health! Shortly after the shooting it was suggested that it was headquarters fingerprint expert Quartermain (who had fired two bullets that evening to the intruder's one) who had accidentally shot McGuire, he being a man with no practical police training. This was denied by the then Minister of Justice John Findlay, but the belief would not go away so easily.

The District Coroner strongly guided his jury that if it so felt that it should state it was not Detective Quartermain who had shot McGuire. The verdict was that McGuire had "died of gunshot wound wilfully inflicted by the person with whom he was grappling" or Pawelka by inference.

The arming of civilians was also copping criticism from all quarters but the police reaffirmed that they had the civilian groups under control. But this proved mistaken the day after the shooting. A quiet tobacconist from Pahiatua, Michael Quirke, brother of Detective Quirke, had officially joined the hunt. After a drunk had pretended to be Pawelka in the Terrace End area of town a rumour was spread that the fugitive was holed up there. Quirke went to Terrace End and was accosted by a Police party. When he ignored or did not hear a challenge and "walked on flourishing a revolver in his hands" he was shot dead by hotel proprietor Henry Overton, a friend of Detective Quirke, also helping in the manhunt.

The rumours that continued to fly were not dispelled by the evidence adduced at Pawelka's subsequent murder trial creating real doubt that Pawelka was responsible. Pawelka was acquitted of McGuire's murder, a verdict most seemed to agree with.

McGuire family lore has it that Quartermain was responsible. Police who had served at the time volunteered that this was the case when interviewed 60 years after.

Pawelka ended up facing a raft of other property charges and was sentenced to 21 years hard labour. This caused a public hue and cry but the Justice Minister held strong and would not allow a reduction in sentence. One could, if one was a cynic, infer that he was also being sentenced for a killing as well. Just a thought.
Pawelka went to prison but that was not the end of this sorry tale. Early on the morning of the 27 August 1911 he escaped from the "condemned cell" at Wellington's Terrace Gaol, never to be seen again in this country. The Pawelka family later confirmed that he hid out in the Kimbolton area until about 15 February 1912 when he went to Auckland and caught a boat headed for Canada. As late as 1963 he was still listed as wanted.

Sergeant McGuire's widow received 500 pound compensation from the government. Not a lot, even in those days, to bring up a young family.

Thieving Police – Dunedin Scandal and More

As a keen amateur student of history, especially New Zealand and Police history I find it fascinating what Police got up to in the old days. As we all know New Zealand's Police has a fine reputation for being overall honest and corrupt-free. Sadly some are led astray and into evil, sometimes by others and sometimes because of their own character flaws.

The following is a story of a group of thieving Constables, with some suspected civilian help, who ran a burglary ring in Dunedin in the early 1900s. It also shows what a lack of effective man management can lead to. It also resulted in the 1905 Commission of Enquiry into the Police. There have been few Commissions of Enquiry into policing in New Zealand, something that says a lot about the honesty and diligence of most police. Each Commission was a result of a period of suspicion and doubt about the activities of certain Police, including, in the 1950s, a Commissioner.

Thomas Moses was born in Cornwall in 1877 and later emigrated to New Zealand with his family. At the age of 13 he was arrested by Detective Thomas Livingstone in Timaru for breaking and entering, being placed on probation for three months. In 1895, at the age of 18 he was again arrested, this time by Detective Terence O'Brien for shop-breaking and received a suspended sentence. Detective Livingstone, the person responsible for arresting baby farmer Minnie Dean, later transferred to Dunedin. Detective O'Brien took promotion and also found himself in Dunedin as District Commander. Both were highly thought of. After Moses's second offence he kept out of trouble and worked on farms until enlisting in the 6th Contingent, New Zealand Mounted Rifles, and going to South Africa where he saw active service as a gunner in the

Permanent Artillery during the Boer War. Upon his return in 1902 he applied for and was accepted into the Police as a Constable. He had produced excellent references from his employers and his application was held over for 16 months while inquiries were made into his application. Amazingly nothing untoward was found of his previous record and his application was successful. At the later Commission of Enquiry arising out of his and others criminal activities in Dunedin it was commented that these earlier convictions would not have stood in his way anyway as they were over the five year time limit of no offending then in force in the Police. In those days it was apparently not unusual for men with previous records to be able to enter the Police if they had been out of trouble for five years at least, depending on the type of offending surely.

Moses was posted to Dunedin and was, understandably, not recognised by O'Brien or Livingstone as the young man they had dealt with years before.

At about this time there seemed to be a relaxation of standards to a certain extent around supervision, allowing Constables more scope for discretion and initiative. Training methods were improving and a belief was afoot that better-educated more rounded men were coming into the police. Perhaps in parallel with the opinion of police management in the 2000s.

This resulted in Sergeants perhaps not being as vigilant in terms of beat supervision and seemed to be a policy encouraged from above. This was to end badly and with the 1905 Commission.

Moses began duty with three other constables, James McDonald, Edward Quill and Oliver Osborne. All four began engaging in burglaries and because of their work as "thief-takers" managed to carry on this side-line for a long time without incurring suspicion. The initial suspicion and line of inquiry was that Moses had, due to his previous criminal behaviour, suborned the others to join him in these activities. The Commission subsequently found the opposite; the other three had been thieving for quite some time and took Moses into their little ring.

Moses was the reason for them being caught though. He paid a visit to his next door neighbour, Robert McQuillan, asking him to store some "wedding presents" for him. The fact that he was on duty and should have been in another part of Dunedin caused the neighbour to be suspicious. McQuillan reported his suspicions to the Police and it went from there. Three of the gang were subsequently convicted and received lengthy sentences with hard labour. Quill, for some reason, was acquitted. McDonald was represented by Alfred Hanlon QC, the most famous barrister in the colony at that time and also the son of a policeman.

Things then began to heat up. The scandal showed that, as well as the four cops, there was an element of the local criminal fraternity involved as well.

Then Commissioner Dinnie's report to the Minister of Police McGowan was wide-ranging in its comments about policing in Dunedin at that time. Sergeants were held "greatly to blame" for the situation, many being too old and inactive to supervise the men under them.

Inspector O'Brien, the District Commander, was alleged by a secret informant, a local businessmen Dinnie approached, to consort with prostitutes and other of the city's "lowest characters" including the rat catcher. Chief Detective Herbert was allegedly a corrupt, drunken, gambling and immoral man who had driven his wife to prostitution. Dunedin's two Commissioned Officers allegedly used junior Constables to "frame" respectable citizens. Dinnie did not pursue these allegations for some reason but it is reported that he believed that there was a "great deal of truth" in them.

Dinnie found that thieving by Police in Dunedin was endemic and well established before O'Brien arrived as District Commander and certainly well before young Moses arrived on the scene. All very messy.

What happened to Constable Quill, the only member of the gang acquitted? He was summarily dismissed, something then commentators called "precious close to a miscarriage of justice".
Dinnie authorised an investigation of local receiver and all round bad guy and night watchman M Reddington's activities and network of police contacts. As a result more Constables were told to resign or they would be sacked. The enforced resignees were given no chance to defend themselves and this provoked outcry from civil libertarians at the time.

It appears that sergeants were replaced, pensioned off and moved on with time but the two officers remained. Over subsequent years applications and outcry were made for reinstatement of the "resigned" constables but to no avail.

Incidents of groups of serving police involved in criminal activity are spread throughout the years and around the country. Constable Alex Ward who served from 1928 to 1966 describes one incident in his memoir (see bibliography) of being stationed at Taranaki Street police station in Wellington in 1932 when two fellow Constables were involved in burglary and theft of goods from warehouses and shops, bringing the goods back to the police station and selling the ill-gotten gains to colleagues. The Constables, Ramm and Stephenson, were in cahoots with a local criminal named Joe White.

Alex tells of having to replace Constable Ramm when he was arrested by detectives while performing point duty at James Smiths corner.

The ensuing inquiry into the actions of the Constables'

colleagues resulted in 90% of the staff stationed at Taranaki Street being in breach of Police Regulations, charged and fined. An interesting outcome. Obviously the Inquiry Team could not prove guilty knowledge on behalf of the police members involved at the time of receiving the goods from the two Constables. Alex's memoirs are quiet on the excuses proffered but he was one of few not charged as he was broke at the time and could not afford the goods offered.

It would be interesting to know what eventually happened to the staff charged. Ramm and Stephenson would have received imprisonment in those days but questions must have hung over the honesty of their colleagues. Such a charge could dog a police officer's career forever.

What is the lesson here? Was it bad supervision or bad selection of staff? It was probably a combination of both.

Rua Kenana – Prophet - Patriot or Traitor?

A sad but true saying is *"Those who cannot remember (**or do not know**) the past are condemned to repeat it."* – George Santayana, philosopher.

What follows is a story containing communication breakdown, ignorance of tikanga, the possible homicides of two men at the hands of Police, allegations of preparation to execute two other men by Police, attempted jury-tampering, intimidation of witnesses, allegations of theft by Police, the list goes on.

In 1907 self-appointed Maori prophet Rua Kenana set up a religious community at the foot of Maungapohatu, the mountain sacred to the people of Tuhoe. Rua believed he was God's appointed successor to Te Kooti, the founder of the Ringatu church. Rua did not have much time for the Crown or for the white man's world and chose to live in isolation. The community had 500 to 600 people at its height. Rua did want communication by way of road and railway with the outside world but the government was not interested. The government of the day was so concerned about him that it based the Tohunga Suppression Act 1907 on him and his activities.

Rua also refused to obey the liquor laws of the day and refused to allow Tuhoe men to enlist in the military during World War 1. This and his statement that he would support the Germans anyway incensed the government to the extent that he was to be dealt with. The fact that his community was thriving and was, by the standards of the day, quite prosperous rankled as well. Rua had sold some land for the equivalent of about $5 million in today's money and was putting this money back into his community. The men also worked on the land for neighbouring farmers and foresters.

The government felt it could not let Rua and his followers continue to be defiant of the liquor laws and the need for conscription when trying to hold a country together during wartime. Rua had spent time in prison in 1915 for liquor offending. His community was simply at odds with what was expected by society then. The men had long hair and Rua had several wives, very much against the social norms of the day.

In January 1916 the government decided to act when Rua was given notice to attend court for sentencing on held over charges from 1911, a type of suspended sentence imposed on liquor offending. He did not attend court asking for a remand due to harvesting. He was convicted in absentia and was fined and sentenced to a term of imprisonment. Sergeant Cummings of Rotorua and District Constable Grant of Te Whaiti tracked Rua down on 12 February 1916 to execute warrants of commitment. He refused to come with them saying that because the state would not give him a liquor licence on the same basis as pakeha, he would not only continue to discourage enlistment but also support the Germans against the British colonisers. It is debatable today what was actually said as the two police did not agree. As a result of this it was decided that Rua had committed sedition. This charge was later thrown out by the Supreme Court due to a conflict of evidence between the police.

Into the story comes Commissioner John Cullen. Cullen was a different kettle of fish, a disciplinarian with very strong views about most things. More about him later. He organised an armed expedition of Police, asking Inspectors around New Zealand to provide "strong athletic constables" including "some suitable men to use the carbines who have served in the Army or the Royal Irish Constabulary". He wanted men who had no compunction killing.

The expedition was organised on military lines with a Commissariat and the Army Medical Corps providing an officer. In the context of the time this could be understandable. Rua's men were well armed due to their lifestyles, NZ was in the middle of a war and did not want any internal rebellions breaking out and one commentator opined that the Police felt that they were expected to do their bit while men of a similar age were fighting in Europe.

It also has to be remembered that the period known as the New Zealand Wars had only stopped in 1872 with Te Kooti's disappearance into the King Country. There had been numerous armed confrontations since between Maori and the Government, surveyors assaulted, and one reportedly murdered by a group of Maori in the King Country, the Parihaka invasion and the Dog Tax War in the Hokianga in the 1890s. Many alive then could remember the campaigns of the NZ Wars or had parents who had fought in these campaigns. When news of the expedition got out civilian groups wanted to join as well to crush the Maori "Rebellion". Their kind offers were declined but they were told if the Police have problems they would be called.
Scary.

The police approached Maungapohatu in three groups, two small groups from Whakatane and Gisborne who were met by Rua and his people on 1 April 1916, welcomed and feasted and the third, very large group from Ruatahuna with Cullen at the head arriving the next day, Sunday 2 April 1916. It all went wrong when Cullen rode straight up to the marae to handcuff Rua. Some warrants could not be executed on Sundays and it was later found that the Police were acting illegally. Rua and his people were preparing to greet and feed Cullen's group with Rua fully intending to surrender to Cullen but still wanting to maintain his mana, however it all went pear-shaped. A shot was fired, most believe by a Constable Arthur Skinner from Tauranga. Rua tried to escape and told his people to scatter. A few Maori fired back. It was the belief of police at the scene that Cullen was "determined to have a shoot-out". Chaos reigned. What started as a few shots soon became pitched battle.

Many Police gave evidence later that, to all intents and purposes, Rua and most of his people were unarmed. During the battle Rua's son Toko Rua and Te Maipi Te Whiu were killed. Te Maipi was shot in the back of the head while running away, unarmed and Toko Rua was overpowered and disarmed then shot in the back. Senior Sergeant Cassells later stated that "Tokorua did not have a gun when I found his body". There was no inquest and the bodies were buried "in great haste".

It was alleged by Rua's people also that two pits were dug and Rua and one other were bound and placed in them by the Police and were to be shot in cold blood but another police member stopped this happening. There seems to have been one senior officer there that day with some common sense. Inspector Sheehan, present that day, from Auckland reportedly suffered in terms of his career for questioning the arrests, the legality and the methods used at Maungapohatu. At least one police member left the force due to not toeing the party line.

After a battle which Cullen describes lasting up to half an hour but was over within a few minutes according to Maori and police witnesses 31 men were arrested under ceasefire, none of them armed. It seems that only a very few of Rua's supporters had armed themselves, two of whom were now dead. Four police had been wounded but all survived with one, William Wright, spending the rest of his career until retirement in 1946 on light duties.

The police stayed at Maungapohatu until 5 April re-enacting the siege for the (reliable) press who accompanied them, overawing the population and allegedly stealing some of their possessions. Only six of those arrested were taken out of Maungapohatu and Rua's trial began on 9 June 2016, at 47 days, the longest trial in New Zealand history until 1977. Apart from charges of sedition and resisting arrest he was charged with several counts including incitement to murder. According to one Constable interviewed many years later but who had been at the scene and had refused to give perjured evidence many police lied during their evidence to protect Cullen. This constable's statement and brief was prepared by Senior Sergeant Cassells but the constable refused to give the evidence, tearing the statement up saying this would have meant he had been instructed to commit perjury. He left the police within a short time. There appeared to be two camps in the police party, pro and anti-Cullen.

Even the pro Cullen police believed that Cassells tried to frame the defendants. The resisting and obstructing charges were dropped as it was held that the Police were not in the lawful execution of their duty that Sunday. Warrants of Commitment could not then be executed on a Sunday. This left the inciting charges and the jury, finding Rua guilty of only "moral resistance" to District Constable Grant and Sergeant Cummings when they visited in the February. They also expressed the clear view as to acquittal. The presiding Judge, Justice Chapman, a friend of Cullen's, then sentenced Rua to twelve months gaol with 18 months reformative detention tacked on. The jury believed Rua was not guilty and the police evidence was unreliable however Rua still got convicted. Cullen later publicly described the jury as "the poorest looking lot I have ever seen in Auckland".

The government had no qualms about this happening but the authorities had egg on their faces due to the police bungling and the acquittals so, to save some face they decided to charge six of Rua's followers with giving perjured evidence at Rua's trial. Prior to the jury being empanelled Cullen wrote to the court "as your present Jury list appears to be packed with Red Feds and other undesirables, I beg to suggest that you get Mr Thomas, the Sheriff, to summon more than double the men usually summoned, so that you may have an opportunity of standing aside such a number of jurymen as will enable you to secure twelve decent men of standing in the district".

The Auckland Crown Solicitor was also replaced by a man adjudged to be better able to secure convictions. Three defendants were later found guilty of perjury and gaoled but in the meantime a defence lawyer was disbarred. After the earlier trial had found the expedition to Maungapohatu had been illegal Rua's people sought compensation. This was denied and they were not given back their confiscated weapons, vital for hunting food. They also had to pay for the cost of the police expedition.

Roll forward nearly 100 years to 2007 when the police undertook an operation to arrest suspected terrorists in the same area of New Zealand. I make no comment on this operation as I was not there, have not studied the files nor interviewed the participants and certainly am not privy to the information police had, most of which could never be released I am sure. Tuhoe has never forgotten Rua and what happened to him and his followers.

Just one comment, did anyone in the police planning team know the saying in the opening line of this story?

Stanley Graham

A man at the end of his tether.

What follows is a tragic tale of a mentally ill man, a loner who his community could not deal with, despite trying. It is also a tale of how New Zealand's Police, prior to the formation of the Armed Offenders Squads in 1963 and the strategy of "cordon, contain and appeal" devised then and still in use today, was expected to approach an armed offender directly, at great risk to themselves and to the public. Eric Stanley "Stan" Graham was New Zealand's first mass killer of the 20th century. He killed seven men, including four police, a civilian and two home guardsmen before he was despatched by a young Auckland Constable when sighted after orders had been given to shoot him on sight, not to call on him.

Graham was born and raised in Kokatahi, New Zealand and as a child, worked at the Longford Hotel, built in 1902, ten miles from Hokitika, whose proprietor was his father, John Graham. Graham met his wife, Dorothy McCoy, when she moved from Rakaia in the late 1920s to work at the Longford Hotel.

They married in Christchurch on 22 December 1930, living there for six months before moving to a dairy property at Kowhitirangi on the West Coast. They were to have two children, a son and a daughter.

Through the late 1930s Graham maintained reasonably good relations with his neighbours, although he and his wife took little part in the district's social life. By 1940 though, the Graham family was under severe financial pressure, having had cream condemned by the Westland Co-operative Dairy Company and having incurred debt from a venture into cattle breeding. As income from his farm dropped, he fell into debt totalling over £550 (approximately NZ$49,263 in 2015). His behaviour took a turn for the worse and he started threatening and abusing neighbours passing his house. Graham and his wife practiced target shooting out the back of their home in the middle of the night. Graham was an expert marksman and experienced hunter and had an assortment of firearms.

During the first part of 1941, Graham was in a dispute with the police, who wanted to relieve him of his .303 rifle for war use. This was finally handed over on 15 July, but Graham and his wife still held a shotgun and two Winchester rifles, a .22 and a .405.

In September, in Christchurch, Mrs Graham purchased, on her husband's behalf, a 7mm Mauser rifle and ammunition. This was the weapon Graham used to shoot his victims.

On 4 October 1941, a neighbour of Graham's, Anker Madsen, complained to Constable Edward Best, stationed in nearby Kaniere, that Graham was accusing him of poisoning his cattle. Best decided not to respond in order to give Graham time to calm himself. On 8 October, Graham confronted Madsen with a rifle. Later that morning, Best attempted to discuss the matter with Graham but backed off with Graham pointing two rifles out the window at him. Best retreated to Hokitika for back-up and returned to the farm with Sergeant William Cooper, 43, and Constables Frederick Jordan, 26, and Percy Tulloch, 35.

After a short conversation inside his house, Graham shot and wounded Sergeant Cooper and Constable Best after Sergeant Cooper apparently reached to disarm Graham. He then fired at Constables Jordan and Tulloch as they ran into the house, killing them both instantly with the one bullet. When the badly wounded Cooper attempted to leave to obtain help, Graham shot him dead on the path in front of the house.

Best was shot once more after allegedly attempting to plead with him, and died three days later. Graham also fatally wounded a field instructor for the Canterbury education board named George Ridley, who had entered Graham's property to assist any wounded along with an armed local, whom Graham threatened and disarmed.

Graham then fled his house, armed with both of his Winchester rifles, his 7mm Mauser Rifle, the .303 rifle taken from the local who had accompanied George Ridley into Graham's property, and a .32 ACP Colt Revolver stolen from Sergeant Cooper's body.

Returning the next evening to discover three members of the Home Guard in his house, Graham opened fire and killed home guardsmen Richard "Maxie" Coulson and Gregory Hutchison in a firefight. During that engagement he was wounded in the right shoulder.

The ensuing manhunt was the biggest in New Zealand history. It was overseen by Commissioner of Police Denis Cummings. More than 100 New Zealand Police and several hundred New Zealand Army and Home Guard personnel searched the area for Graham for 12 days with orders to shoot on sight if they found Graham still armed.

On 10 October, both of Graham's Winchester rifles and 800 rounds of ammunition were discovered. Blood was discovered on one of the rifles, suggesting he was wounded.

In the next few days, Graham's blood-soaked shirt and the .303 rifle he had stolen earlier were recovered, and after 9 October, he was sighted numerous times by home guardsmen and civilians alike, and on at least three occasions he was fired upon whilst attempting to return to his home or whilst simply walking in the vicinity of it. On at least two occasions, cattle on nearby farms were found slashed or shot, and on at least one occasion, a dead heifer was found with meat taken from it.

On 17 October, a farmhouse belonging to Henry Growcott, a childhood friend of Graham's, was broken into and food was taken. On 20 October, parties of police were positioned around his home, expecting Graham to return to the Growcott farm. In the middle of the night, after being spotted by two police constables and a local civilian carrying his rifle and ammunition belts, an injured Graham was shot by Auckland Constable James D'Arcy Quirke with a .303 rifle from a distance of 25 metres as he crawled through a patch of scrub. After being shot, he was surrounded by almost a hundred police and army personnel, reportedly telling one of them that he "could have shot some more". He died the following morning at approximately 5:25 a.m. at Westland Hospital, Hokitika, the same hospital where Constable Best had succumbed to his injuries. He was buried at Hokitika Cemetery. Constable Quirke reported that Graham told him he was intending to give up that night.

Later that month, the Graham property was burnt to the ground and Mrs Graham and her children left the area.

This all took place during wartime and the Nazi propagandist Lord Haw Haw claimed that Adolf Hitler had sent Graham a telegram "Hold the South Island. Am sending another man to take the North Island".

Rumours (mistakenly) abounded after the tragedy that Constable Quirke, who had only been in the police 13 months, was believed to have resigned because of the effects of being identified as the man who shot Graham. As a consequence the names of police who have since shot offenders have been withheld from publication, a practice that is constantly under attack today by civil liberties and lawyers. It took another 22 years and the lives of five more police and a traffic inspector plus several being seriously wounded before the tactic of the direct approach was abandoned for the more measured and careful methods used today.

At the time of the shooting Graham's hamlet was known as Koiterangi. The name has changed to Kowhitirangi since. I have read research that gives the reason for the change as the tragedy but I am not sure if that is correct. The likely reason is that local Iwi asked for the name change, believing Koiterangi a corruption of the name.

Slain on duty – Police after Koiterangi

The years following the tragic events at Koiterangi in 1941, resulting in the deaths of four police, three civilians and the offender, were turmoil for senior police in terms of dealing with armed offenders.

The fallout of the Stanley Graham affair haunted the police for over 20 years before. following pressure from the public and the press together with war-experienced senior officers, the Armed Offenders Squad was formed in 1964. Between Graham's death in 1941 and the squad's formation a further five police and a traffic officer were to die, shot on duty, and many more wounded by deranged gunmen.

For some reason sections of the public and the press vilified the police over Graham's death and tried to make Graham a hero instead of the homicidal maniac he was. Graham's shooter, a young Auckland Constable, was named in the press and received unbearable pressure and criticism for his actions at Koiterangi. He put his head down and just got on with his career.

The administration of the police forbade police attending armed offender incidents to either shoot the offender or return fire in an effort to apprehend the offender. This resulted, in one incident on 21 December 1960 when Arthur McQuoid, an expert marksman with a long history of violence, absconded from the Papakura Courthouse and took refuge with a rifle on the top of a sawdust extractor tower at a timber yard where he worked. From there he shot at everything that moved in the near vicinity. The officer in Charge at the scene refused to allow the attending police, including members of the armed Auckland Consorting Squad, to shoot the offender, instead ordering them to try to knock him down with firehoses. This really enraged McQuoid who then began to shoot very accurately, puncturing the fire hoses and wounding five police and one fireman. After two hours he got bored and shot himself, solving the problem.

Other than awards given to the attending police nothing further was done to stop the administration's callous disregard for police lives. It was reported by Bill Brien, a highly respected and senior detective, that during the incident the officer in charge was more worried about the hubcap on one of the police cars being hit by McQuoid.

In those days Detectives had ready access to weapons as needed and the Auckland Consorting Squad was armed full time as an informal pseudo Armed Offender Squad but with no deep training in tactics or planning or any special equipment. I guess the rest of New Zealand just made do with what they had.

Earlier incidents were of note. In 1949 a depressed air force member at Weedons Air Force base holed up on the grounds and began shooting at everyone in sight. He was eventually shot dead by someone, either Police or Air Force as both groups returned intensive fire. The scene was such a mess forensics could not work out whose bullet actually killed the guy.

At 8.30 p.m. on 31 January 1949 Traffic Inspector John Kehoe was in the main street of Whakatane when he saw a motorcycle ridden by Richard Angus McGill pass him at normal speed and then return at 60 mph. Kehoe chased McGill until he stopped at Poroporo where McGill shot Kehoe several times with a .38 pistol, killing him. McGill's body was later found in an orchard at Awakeri where he had shot himself. With the body were two revolvers, a pistol and 75 rounds of ammunition. McGill had a strong interest in firearms.

On 27 May 1951 Sergeant W S Hughes was shot dead at Otaki when he tried to apprehend an armed youth following a domestic dispute. Noema Raana Rika had been arguing with Mrs Mary Te Hiwi in the dilapidated shack they lived in at Otaki. Mrs Te Hiwi was concerned about the attention Rika was paying to her 16 year old daughter Victoria. Mrs Te Hiwi's other daughter Pearl France was also at the shack trying to take Victoria back to Wellington to live with her. Rika, angry with the women for trying to leave fired two shots from a shotgun at the house. Sergeant Hughes and two men visited the scene but Rika had gone.

Later in the afternoon Hughes returned as he had had a report Rika was back at the house. He waited outside while the women packed. Rika, lying in nearby long grass, fired a shot at Hughes, striking him in the left wrist, badly wounding him. All three women and Sergeant Hughes all rushed inside the house and barricaded the door. Some other children staying at the house jumped out of a window and escaped with Rika firing shots at them. Rika managed to gain entry to the house and shot all four occupants to death. It appeared that because of the wrist wound Sergeant Hughes had been unable to fire his .32 pistol. It was empty when found and it appears Mrs Te Hiwi and Mrs France may have fired shots from it in an attempt to save themselves. After killing the three women and Sergeant Hughes, Rika shot himself.

aIn 1953 Detective B D Christofferson was awarded the George Medal after being gravely wounded arresting an armed youth. He had earlier apprehended a youth wanted for shop breaking and accompanied him back to the boy's home to search it. He could not gain access to a shed as it was locked. The youth decamped and returned with another lad, both armed with rifles. Christofferson and the father of the boy had entered the shed and found weapons and ammunition. The boys held the two at gunpoint. One boy went to the back of the house whereupon Christofferson heard a woman screaming. Without thought of his own safety he rushed to the area to save the woman. He was shot by both offenders, tackling one in the process, receiving grave wounds. Both boys left and were later arrested by other police in a car. Christofferson recovered eventually.

It seems to have been expected of attending police that they sacrifice themselves if needed for the safety of the public and even the offender but that they were not to return fire.

Other such incidents occurred during the 1940s, 1950s and early 1960s until two tragedies within a month, together with pressure from the press, the public and serving police, made senior police re-think tactics.

On 6 January 1963 Victor George Wasmuth, a resident of the Waitakeres, near Auckland, shot and wounded a member of the public visiting a next door dog kennel to uplift his dog. He then shot and killed the kennel owner. Detectives attended under the command of Detective Inspector Wallace Chalmers. Chalmers had been involved in the Graham tragedy in 1941 and was clearly afraid of bringing the police into disrepute. He instructed police to only shoot to wound. Detective Sergeant N Power was shot and killed when he approached Wasmuth's house with a loaded tear gas pistol, trying to fire it. He had not released the safety catch, dying probably due to his lack of training. Another constable tried to fire at Wasmuth but his gun jammed, again lack of training. Then Chalmers was shot and killed after shouting a warning to another constable, giving away his position to Wasmuth.

Wasmuth was eventually wounded and overpowered. He was found unfit to plead and committed. Wasmuth had a feral and deep hatred of the police to the extent that, when police had to visit the National Secure Unit at Lake Alice it was advised that they wear plainclothes. The sight of a police uniform used to send Wasmuth up the wall. He died in care.

On 3rd February 1963, a fine summer's evening, less than a month after the above incident, two young cops, Constables James Richardson and Bryan Schultz, attended a reported domestic dispute at an address in Herbert Street, Lower Hutt. They pulled up outside the old villa and three shots rang out before Schultz could turn the ignition off. The first shot hit Richardson in the head, the second hit the car door and the third hit Schultz in the chest, killing both men instantly. The range from the lounge window where the shooter was waiting was less than 20 feet. The offender Bruce Douglas McPhee tried to leave the house by the front door but was apprehended by two bystanders, being taken into custody by the deceased's section mates Constables Doug Mawson and Tata Parata within minutes of their arrival at the scene.

The photos of this crime will be indelibly printed into the minds of all graduating police who were posted to Lower Hutt for many years after this tragedy. Upon reporting for duty we were given a lecture on how domestic disputes are attended in the Hutt area and then taken upstairs to the photo lab and shown the crime photos of the homicide. Looking at the bodies of two young cops wearing, in those days, the same uniform I was wearing 8 years later was a very sobering experience for a 19 year old. Growing up in the Hutt I knew the story anyway as in those days violence was not as common.

McPhee was released after 11 years for double murder and lived in Stokes Valley upon parole. Older members of the station were livid at the light sentence he received for cold-bloodedly shooting two unarmed men. Both Doug and Tata were still working at the Hutt. Time is silent on what their thoughts were, but knowing both men well as quiet men I guess they struggled.

Thanks to the likes of ex-Commissioner Bob Walton and a few other far-sighted senior officers it was realised that things had to change. The police were not to be just untrained, lightly armed targets for murderers. Thus began the Armed Offenders Squad in 1964, still today using the basic tactic of Cordon, Contain and Appeal it has always used with outstanding success. Unfortunately police have continued to be slain in the course of their duty but they are now not expected to sacrifice themselves for some greater good.

A Family Tragedy- Detective Inspector James Murray

Growing up in the Hutt in the late 50s and early 60s I occasionally overheard adult conversations concerning a cop who shot all his family in Myrtle Crescent, Lower Hutt. As was normal in those days, when adults became aware little ears were wagging the subject was usually changed so I never really got a handle on the mystery. Being of a curious nature and always up for a good story I would ask questions about this and promptly be told to "go outside and play" or some such adult dismissal of a nosey kid.

Years later when stationed in the Hutt as a young Constable I would again overhear snatches of conversation amongst the older staff of what seemed to be an awful tragedy. Discussion was not encouraged so the story went to the back of my mind where it resided for over 40 odd years until I read about the very sad incident in Sherwood Young's very good book called "With Confidence and Pride", a history of policing in the Wellington District published in 1994.

I would like to retell it here as it is a sad story of a man who was obviously at the end of his tether. It is a tale that shows that no matter who we are or our position in society, we all have a breaking point. It is also timeless and relevant to today's pressured life.
T
he Police and public alike were shocked to hear of a tragedy in 1958 that involved one of the Lower Hutt Police staff. Shortly before noon on Sunday 9th March tennis players at the Hutt Tennis Club were startled when they heard a woman calling for help over a fence from a house in Myrtle Crescent.

Blood was streaming from a wound in her face. Inside her home the players found the bodies of two men. They had both been shot. Sergeant Louis Belmont Vasta and a Constable were the first to arrive (the Hutt station would have been about 200 metres away). Lying on the floor of a passageway near the front door was the body of Detective Inspector James Jeremiah Murray, his police .32 calibre automatic pistol still in his hand. In a doorway of one of the rooms was the body of Robert F. Black, Murray's father in law. A third body, that of Detective Murray's 18 year old son Richard, was later found on a bed in another room.

At the inquest it was determined that Inspector Murray had been worried about the sale of his house and that his distress had been compounded by the recent death of his brother. The Court also heard that Inspector Murray, the relieving officer in charge of the Wellington CIB, had suffered poor physical health for the previous three years and that an expected promotion had not gone ahead. The Coroner's verdict was that Inspector Murray had shot and killed his son and father-in-law and then turned the weapon on himself 'while the balance of his mind was disturbed'. The first shot, fired at Mrs Murray, had ricocheted off her jaw and exited through her cheek. The pistol was found to have jammed as Inspector Murray had fired his last shot.

The Ultimate Decision - Shoot - Don't Shoot

The lives of police are stalked by tragedy; such is the nature of the role they took an oath to uphold as Constables. They are not alone in this, medical staff, and other emergency service personnel live with death every day of their lives. The not-so-subtle difference between police and these other services is that police also often die or are severely injured in the course of their duties. Thankfully this is rare in New Zealand, but sadly, perhaps, becoming less rare as our society becomes more violent and less caring.

Since 1886 there have been 30 New Zealand police slain by another whilst on duty. All but one of the homicides have been resolved by either the offender being arrested and charged with murder, slain by Police or taking his own life. The killer of Constable James Dorgan at Timaru in 1921 eluded capture after an extensive investigation.

George Pawelka of Palmerston North was acquitted of a charge of murdering Sergeant John Maguire in 1910 following trial, the case remaining unresolved. A further list of police who died, on duty by non-criminal causes is, at the time of writing, 19, but is very incomplete with research still underway to identify the full number, expected to be quite high.

These figures do not account for the number of police who were permanently disabled or died prematurely due to wounds or injuries, of whom there have been many as well.

There were police deaths prior to 1886 in the provincial police and the Armed Constabulary, especially during the New Zealand Wars but these are a separate record from the New Zealand Police Force founded in 1886. Also the Armed Constabulary members, although holding the rank of Constable, were more soldiers than police.

Since 1886 New Zealand's police, a normally unarmed service, but with ready access to weapons, has shot and killed well over 40 people. The numbers are difficult to define but would include Rua Kenana's son Toko Rua and associate Te Maipi Te Whiu in 1916 and Stanley Graham in 1941. Police having to use ultimate force is becoming more common as time goes by sadly as criminals are now more armed than at any time in modern New Zealand history and are more willing to use firearms against police or associates.

Following Stanley Graham's shooting in 1941 history shows that, for the next 23 years, the police almost had a policy of never shooting and were expected to arrest an armed offender without using weapons. As stated above there was some cost in lives and serious injury in this time.

The police who shot Toko Rua and Te Maipi Te Whiu have not been identified in history texts although one or two individual police on the raid figured prominently in the fire-fight and were named. The officer who shot Stanley Graham was named in 1941, Constable James D'Arcy Quirke from Auckland. It is reported that he was somewhat hounded by the press and the public following the shooting. He remained in the police for some years after the shooting, not forced out as some anecdotes portray.

Since that time, and especially since the formation of the Armed Offenders Squads in 1964, police who shoot retain anonymity and are protected from publicity. There has been only one exception, with, eventually, an outcome for the Constable involved following the shooting of Steven Wallace in Waitara in 2000 and the subsequent private prosecution undertaken by

Wallace's family against the Constable who was acquitted of murder and who remained in the police but stationed elsewhere in New Zealand.

Police involved in shootings are known by numbers or letters of the alphabet, whatever the Officer in Charge of the subsequent homicide investigation feels is needed. Throughout any following inquiries into a police shooting the participants are only known by these letters or numbers. Court orders are made suppressing the identity of police. These orders are made for several reasons but obviously the safety of the officer or officers concerned and their families is paramount.

No police officer in New Zealand goes to work to kill a person but there are sadly occasions when police have to resort to such action to protect themselves or any member of the public in danger of death or serious injury at the hands of a criminal suspect. The lives of police who pull the trigger are changed forever. New Zealand police are not soldiers and are not trained to kill unless under the provisions of the law around self-defence and the Police current policy regarding use of force. Such an action is very much a last resort and, usually, a decision made in a moment, a decision that will be picked to pieces by a subsequent homicide investigation, a possible court case and the Coroner as well as the Independent Police conduct Authority, a Judge, who acts totally separate from the courts and police in deciding whether or not a shooting was justified.

The full weight of the state falls on the shoulders of any police officer who pulls the trigger, shooting a suspect. This is a worrying time for the officer concerned and a terrible time for the suspect's family.

Nowadays police who shoot have access to counselling and

other support, if needed. They will be sheltered from the press and public for the reasons above. For some officers it begins the end of their career, for others they will move on in the police. All will have the memories of course.

Whilst writing this book I approached two ex-colleagues who were forced to make the ultimate decision to shoot as Constables, asking both if they would like to share their experiences in this book. Both left the police many years ago and no longer live in New Zealand, having not done so for some time. Both were, in their time, very good officers and I still consider them friends.
T
here will be no names in the next two chapters and I will use writer's licence to change any details to guard their anonymity. When reading these accounts, please understand that matters of recall and the trauma of events can affect memory many years later. The shootings were many years apart and perhaps show the difference in the way the men were treated by the police administration.

The Story of "One"

Many years ago I was working as a Detective when I received a file to investigate concerning a burglary at the local picture theatre where the safe had been forced open and the contents stolen.

That period in time saw crime fairly rampant in the our area with most of the serious crime being committed by a relatively small number of hardened criminals and of course 'A' was one of them.

When I received the file, I prioritized it as urgent and made a fairly long list of suspects to work through.

It was only a matter of a couple of days of talking to some of the suspects on my list that it became apparent 'A' was the likely offender and because it was getting very close to Xmas I was keen to locate and interview him.

Before I had the chance to do so, I was called out from home early to assist in an enquiry concerning the earlier stabbing death of a man in a nightclub some 5 or 6 hours earlier.

During the briefing 'A' was nominated as a suspect and I made my situation concerning him known to the briefing.
Mainly because of this I was placed on the suspect team and was joined by another Detective. As soon as the briefing was completed he and I (and maybe another D??) made our way out to start looking for 'A' On the way we received notification via radio that more witnesses had revealed that 'A' was definitely responsible for killing the victim.

We started visiting some of his known haunts without too much success when a little later in the morning we heard a radio transmission that 'A' was at the local tip talking to a council worker.

We were not too far away so put the pedal to the metal and got up to the tip in time to see 'A' driving his open roofed Landrover on the way out. We managed to get behind him and made numerous loud hailer calls for him to stop but of course he wasn't having a bar of that.

As we drove down from the main tip face toward the entry/exit gate a rubbish truck started backing up of the road to block his escape but he managed to just sneak around the back of it with inches to spare. (I have no idea who arranged the truck attempt)

Once we got out of the tip the 'great chase' began. Pretty sure we were directly behind 'A' as I recall and continually making appeals for him to pull over and stop but there was no way he was going to do so.. I recall heading south and looking behind me and seeing a great line up of Police vehicles with the uniform cars activating their blue flashing lights. Can't recall how many vehicles there were, more than a dozen? but we had a bit of a laugh and commented about how the 'chase' was turning into a bit of an American farce.

We weren't going particularly fast but on occasion 'A' overtook a slower vehicle which resulted in him glancing off and colliding with some oncoming cars. I can still recall the looks of utter bewilderment on the faces of the affected drivers and we continued on our way.

We tried to get alongside 'A' a couple of times but oncoming vehicles prevented that happening...

We heard on the radio that a cop in a patrol car was going to try and provide a rolling block and hopefully get this guy stopped. I saw the cop attempt his rolling stop but 'A' just rammed the rear of his patrol car.

At some point the Landrover veered off the road onto the shingle of the local river.

We were in a commodore car and I recall thinking 'we are stuffed now, he will be off into the hills and we would need air support or another four wheel vehicle to catch him.

When we got onto the shingle we got out of the car and pretty much watched him drive through the water. We were only 20 – 30 metres behind him and were pretty pissed off at that stage that he was getting away.

He drove through the river which wasn't really that deep, maybe only 4 – 500mm and flowing pretty slowly.

At that point I though oh well I better get over there and try to chase on foot, pissed off that I was going to get a wet arse. Feet anyway! Over the next several seconds additional police vehicles arrived on the scene and I was surprised to see Sunray arrive. (Boss of the local CIB) Pretty much at the same time the Landrover drove out of the water and stopped on the riverbank. I have no idea why

At the time I was a member of the local AOS but was unarmed.

I heard Sunray yell out '…. shoot the tyres out'

I guess he was concerned, as was I, that 'A' was going to get his vehicle going again and bugger off. We certainly did not want him on the run in a desperate state hurting anyone else. It was likely a fairly safe bet that some innocent would get in his way.

Someone handed me a police issue rifle (think it was a Sako .223) and I heard Sunray again yell out 'Shoot the tyres out'

I actually said to everyone around me that it probably wasn't going to be of any great benefit shooting. I had reservations on a couple of areas...

The tyres were of a decent treaded off road type and I thought the chances of the round penetrating were pretty slim. I also didn't have a great deal of exposed sidewheel of the tyre and given the angle I had to fire on the chances of the round just ricocheting off was pretty high..

The third concern I had was 'Where has this rifle come from and how good are the sights ?? I didn't have a clue but figured it would not be accurate... I desperately wished I had my own AOS weapon!! Bear in mind all this happened in a matter of a few seconds...

'A' was still sitting in the Landrover, trying, I presume, to get it started or moving again.

I lay in the prone position of the riverbed (a rip sound – there goes my nice suit!) I took aim at the greatest visible area of the inside wall of the left side rear tyre pretty much level with the centre or level of the axle and fired...

I saw the vehicle shudder ever so slightly but I couldn't say if the tyre had been penetrated. Almost immediately after the shot 'A' got out of the vehicle on the driver's side and was carrying a large axe.

I thought "this is going to be interesting" and chambered another round thinking that perhaps he was going to advance on myself and other members who were standing nearby...

Pretty much as soon as I chambered the round I saw out the corner of my eye a chopper coming in to the area and I watched it land on the same side of the riverbank that 'A' was on, maybe 20 – 30 metres from his then position at the back of the Landrover.

I watched a Police dog handler get out of the chopper with his dog. Pretty sure the chopper then took off.

I thought at the time that we were in for a front and centre view of 'A' being taken down by the dog but in an instant he flung the axe through the air toward the handler.

At the time my thoughts were going 100 miles an hour. First thought was.. is the dog going to get him or am I going to have to engage him? You know how that goes looking down the barrel Ratts..

Then in the instant I saw the axe hit the handler in the head and before I could even reconcile that, he was firing his revolver at 'A'. He had a .38 Smith and Wesson and I remember thinking, gee there's a bit length of space between them and I wondered what impact the rounds were going to have on 'A' if he is hit.

I counted the six rounds fired and saw 'A' go down. My immediate thought was bloody hell, how many times was he hit?? In a really surreal moment at the time Sunray said '...., make a notebook entry right now!

I thought gee that's a bit weird but yes I can see and appreciate the value in doing so. I handed the rifle off to someone and leaning on one of the patrol cars made a notebook entry of events from when we arrived at the tip until the chase was over with 'A' dead.

When I was doing this I saw another detective and the

handler walk past. The handler was bleeding fairly profusely from a forehead wound and assisted along by the detective.

A short time later I was approached by Sunray who was with another commissioned officer and asked for my notebook which I handed over. He gave it to this other officer who read it and then made a really smart comment which was along the lines of ... "that was really efficient of you to make such a contemporaneous notebook entry Detective"

I thought you fucking wanker, what's your agenda?

I also wondered at the time why Sunray asked (ordered) me to make the entry then and there???

It was only a few minutes after this I was told that someone would take me back to the station to make a more 'in depth' report.

On arrival at the station I was met in the yard by a Uniform Branch Senior Sergeant who told me to report to Sunray's office where I was to be interviewed by a senior officer. The old cogs were starting to move around again and I thought 'what the fuck is going on here..?)

Anyway I go into Sunray's office and Detective Superintendent ..... is sitting in the chair.

He asks me a series of questions pretty much starting from the early morning briefing in Wellington and I started getting a bit uncomfortable.

I told him so and said it was starting to look a bit like I was a suspect for something..? I wasn't a bit comfortable and told him I didn't much like the way the interview was going and I probably would not be saying much else. He gave me the usual bullshit about oh we are going trying to get to the facts of the matter blah blah

Anyway I told him that if he wanted to speak to me further then maybe I would do so with a rep from the police association or even my solicitor.. I was pretty pissed off at that point and couldn't understand what the hell was going on.

I went back to my office and started making a more in-depth report for Sunray who I knew had my back.

An hour or two later the Landrover was bought into the yard on the back of a truck and I was asked to have a look at it, specifically the left hand rear tyre. There were a number of personnel present but I can't for the life of me remember who they were. I'm pretty sure the Detective Superintendent was there and everybody was inspecting the vehicle.

I was asked to look at the wheel and make any comments I had. I had a look at it and obviously the vehicle had been moved around a bit but I saw what I thought was a bullet impact point on the sidewall together with evidence on the rim that the round had ricochetted into it.

No drama I thought…

Then someone said 'you shot him in the leg …'

I said I did not however there was a very remote possibility that his leg was hit by the ricochet however I could not see any evidence of this.

(Turns out he was shot in the leg but not his good one and it was later learned that the slug was from a .38!) Wankers. Talk about jumping to all the wrong conclusions early on and making me feel like a bloody crim.

Later in the day we had a small gathering in the CIB main office to celebrate Xmas but it was a pretty sombre occasion for me and I went home a lot earlier than I normally would.

I actually forgot to put a bit in the story which I pondered on at the time of the shooting and for a fair period after. I always wondered that if I had not fired that first shot whether the outcome would have been the same for 'A' and the handler.

My reasoning was that after the shot was fired 'A' had any number of thoughts running through his head and probably was correct that he was certainly under attack and needed to do something about it thus throwing the axe at the handler.

Who knows, but I certainly held that question in my mind for a few years, probably still do.

Sometime after the shooting I was invited to join another section of the Police and I remained there until resigning a few years later, As far as support went for anything mate it didn't as you know.

A fair while after 'A' was in the ground I got a call from someone (can't even remember who it was) telling me that the slug in his leg came from a .38 and not my .223. Thanks I said.

The Story of "Two"

I first started my stint in law enforcement at age 21 by joining the Ministry of Transport. I remained with the MOT for 9 years then resigned to join the NZ police. I went through 6 months of police training to be posted to a mid-sized city.

I really enjoyed the police constable role; my entire time was spent in uniform branch, jobs varied between sectional duties in the city, to policing in rural areas, first relieving in small stations, then being posted to a small station. Consisting of a Sgt, 6 constables and 1 CIB member, we worked day and late shifts. The station was unmanned after hours but was covered by the city station approximately 20kms away. We were not on call.

I had also been a member of the Armed Offenders Squad for 13 years. I continued with the squad while I worked in the small station.

At the time I was married with 2 children aged 5 and 6yrs. My wife worked part time as a nurse in the neighboring city. We had a enjoyable life style. Baby sitters were on call when ever our shifts clashed. The children were attending a rural school. We enjoyed the small town life, I joined the local volunteer fire brigade to help them out with their day time manning problems. We were loyal to the small town, we did all our shopping there, we banked there, bought cars there, it was a close friendly little town. I had intended to retire there.

Then one evening, I had just completed afternoon shift, a really quiet uneventful shift. At 11pm I went home and went to bed. At about 3am I was awoken by a phone call from police coms. I was asked if I would mind checking out some disorder in the town. Very unusual to be called back to duty, the first and only time it had occurred. Although I was not officially on duty or on call, I agreed to attend. I was also told that a patrol from the neighbouring city had been dispatched.

The ensuing incident changed my life and the life of my family. The nice easy times were about to come to an end. The incident resulted in an armed confrontation, a confrontation every police officer dreads, and hopes will never happen to them. I shot in self-defence, killing the offender. The following years have been the most unbelievable, the most trying time a police officer could ever imagine.

From the day of the shooting our tight family unit was moved out of our nice warm secure home we had owned, where 2 children were born and raised. We never returned, it was locked up and abandoned. In the police's wisdom my family and I were moved to a secure location. Because of threats to myself and the family it was deemed unsafe to remain in the family home, or the town. We were moved between motels and safe houses. I was stood down from police duties for this period while the police investigation was under way. This carried on for approximately 6 months, the house was subsequently sold for us.

Finally I was transferred out of the area, to another posting in a larger city. It was a relief to get away from the region, as I was forever checking my back.

We moved to a small town. I commenced police duties in a nearby city. Things were progressing well. The children recommenced their schooling, my wife found another job. Then about 12 months later I was advised of charges being laid against me, murder and manslaughter. I was immediately stood down again while preparing for the preliminary hearing.

My first day in court was utterly mind shattering, it is not what I had ever imagined, I could remember walking through the court room towards the dock. I was in a stunned state of shock, my protection officer behind me telling me where to go, left, left right etc. It was the court room where I had worked regularly, but on the day of my appearance, I was totally lost.

The subsequent hearing lasted 6 weeks. Charges against me were dismissed. Wow! I thought, time to get back to normality. But it didn't last, an appeal resulted in fresh charges being reinstated. My time in High Court loomed. I was stood down from police duties once again.

High Court was scheduled for about 6 months' time.

High Court progressed well. It lasted about 6 days. Many highs and lows. Former police officers who claimed to be experts gave evidence against me. Their few minutes of fame was brief.

My well-prepared defence lawyer tore them to shreds. Towards the end of the hearing, while the jury were out deliberating, I met with the then current Police Commissioner in an adjoining courtroom. He handed me a personal letter. A letter that I still have today and cherish.

His support throughout the whole ordeal had been overwhelming. I am sure that had I made the wrong decision on the night, I would have been hung out to dry.

Finally I was found not guilty, a huge relief, time to get back to reality.

I remained in policing for approximately 10 more years, before deciding to relocate outside of New Zealand. During these 10 years a Coroners hearing was held, an investigation and report by the

Independent Police Complaints Authority, and a civil case was heard.

In the early days I had a meeting with another police officer who had been in the same position as myself. He said to me that, it would take about 6 years before the horrors of reliving the event to finally fade. He was right, but it only faded. Not a day would pass without me reliving that event. I would go over in my mind different scenarios, what if I had done this or what if I had done that, played over and over in my mind.

Incidentally, every 12 months on the anniversary of the event, at the same time (about 3 - 4am) I would wake momentarily, I would take a moment, then go back to sleep.

I think also of the family of the victim, they have endured sad and hard times themselves. This incident was over 20 years ago, but it still continues to haunt me. It will continue to haunt me for many years to come.

There is so much more to this story. The bid to remain anonymous and need for name suppression. The stress, the many visits to a psychologist, and the safety and well-being of my family. The cost to me and my family have been absolutely horrendous. I did what I had been trained to do, I did what I was expected to do, I reacted in self-defence and I survived. Many police officers will face the same decision. My only words of advice to them is, think wisely, be so sure of your actions, get it right.

Throughout this ordeal, my wife remained the absolute loyal supporter. Sadly the marriage did not last.

History of Police training in New Zealand

"Training is the process that molds the individual to meet the demands of the police service. Over the years methods and venues may have changed, but there have been two powerful elements of training – ensuring that the trainee knows the elements of police law and practice, and modelling for him or her the appropriate behavior expected by superiors and colleagues" – Peggy Gordon, well-known police educator.

Memories of basic police training at the Lyttleton Depot, Trentham Training School or Porirua Police College are usually a mixture of great, not-so-great and sobering. Most alive today who have served or are serving in the Police have had the benefit of a decent police training scheme in all its different hues, places and shapes. This was not always the case in the history of the New Zealand Police and its antecedents, the Armed Constabulary, Provincial Police Forces and the New Zealand Constabulary.

The original police training courses in the late 1860s also included road building, military drills and preparation for war against insurgent "rebels". Any actual police training usually only occurred if or when AC or Constabulary Force officers based at the Mt Cook training base in Wellington were asked to help the local Wellington Provincial Police Force as needed, training learnt on the job from another Constable, usually not that well trained either.

Over the years, depending on the attitude of the then Commissioner, training waxed and waned for Police recruits. During war time any Police training scheme was placed on hold due to a drop off in recruiting. Many police employed during war time did not enjoy formal training and may not have been up to the usual standard anyway as all fit and able men were at war. During World

War 1 the Police actually re-employed retired or discharged members, some in their sixties, with mixed results.

Policing was very much a working class career for men in the late 19th and early 20th century with a few well-educated men joining and rapidly climbing the ranks. Most recruits came from manual and farming occupations and usually earnt less than what they could in civvy street. They were also required to work seven days per week, this only dropping to six days per week in 1937, causing protest from conservative serving members.

Venues for training have varied over the years from the Armed Constabulary base on the top of Mt Cook in Wellington to the old Mt Cook Police station, still in situ in Buckle Street, to Wellington South Police station and complex in Rintoul Street. Many Wellington readers will remember this base, the dog section, garage, in-service training and driving school were based there in later years but it was also the horse training area for the Mounted Police up until the late thirties. Wellington South closed and opened more regularly than a public bar at times depending on finance, manpower requirements, war and the varying whims of Commissioners. There seemed to be an underlying wish to not have a Police service that was too bright or well-educated in the early days for some reason. Wellington South operated off and on from 1909 to 1953 when it closed as training moved temporarily to the Lyttleton Navy barracks prior to the Police Training School opening in Trentham in February 1956.

In 1937, following a particular recruiting drive, two Police courses were run at Trentham Army Camp but members had to be dressed in military uniform and operate under military rules. They were also required to do road-building and work in the local gravel pit. Perhaps the Army thought they were getting an Armed Constabulary back again!

The influence of military training in the New Zealand Police has its genesis in the foundations of policing in New Zealand, the service falling out of a split between the military and civil wings of the Constabulary Force in 1886. Most, if not all, new recruits at that time came from the Permanent Artillery with civilians only being recruited from 1896.

In terms of education standards recruits were required to pass the Standard 4 level by the end of their course in 1902. In new money Standard Four is year six. As years went by the education standards increased along with the general raising of education standards in the community. It has to be remembered that New Zealand did not have universal secondary education until at least the late 1940s with most children leaving school after standard six or year eight.

Literacy and numeracy were particular problems for many years until the Police began entrance exams in about 1955. At that time the recruit had to have two years secondary education and be able to pass the entry exams, a situation that still existed when I joined in 1970 although it was "expected" that cadet entrants would have at least School Certificate. Other criteria came into play if an entrant did not, trade qualifications and life experience, previous military or police service for recruits were all taken into account.

By 1939 training had really taken off and the quality of recruit passing out of the Depot was "excellent" but the coming war put the kibosh on that, training having to stop until May 1946 when Wellington South re-opened.

Around this time it was recognized that the Police needed to also provide ongoing education to its trainees in subjects other than law and practice. Thus began the era of the civilian instructor and broadened the knowledge base of young constables coming out of training, studying subjects such as Sociology, English, Mathematics and Geography and undertaking typing and drafting training for maps.

Although approval for the recruitment of women into the police was gained in 1938 none was employed until 1941, 10 officers attached to the Detective Branch for work with young women and girls. Their training was held separately in Wellington South and they were accommodated in private bed and breakfast outlets while the boys lived in barracks. It was 1956 before men and women trained together and 1972 before women police lost the designation "Women's Division" or "WD" and could be deployed on a full range of police duties. The term "WD" hung around for years though more as a compliment than not.

I recall as a young cop in the early 1970s talking to old codgers who had been working since the war and told of times when cops walked the beat for months before they got to the "depot". They just operated on common sense and under the strong supervision of older constables and tough old sergeants. Very much a "sink or swim" time by the sound of it.

The police found themselves back at Trentham Army Camp, but on their terms, in 1956 when the new Police Training School opened. At the time I went through we also had the Ministry Of Transport School opposite on the other side of the parade ground and we intermingled with their trainees at meal times. When the Police moved to Porirua in 1981 it was proposed that the MOT also move into the college but they decided to stay at Trentham in a new building. They eventually arrived in 1992 but not as they would have planned or probably preferred at the time, but as part of the police following the merger of the police and MOT staff early that year.

Cadets started training in 1957 with the Holland Wing. The Police were keen to capture young men, "the cream of secondary school students" (not my words) straight from college and this solved the problem. Cadets joined at 17, completed 19 months training but did not become attested Probationary Constables until they turned 19, a few younger ones working for some months after graduation as Temporary Constables. With the advent of society expecting children to remain at school until seventh form or Year 13 the Cadet system ceased to be relevant and was canned in 1982. Girls were not employed as cadets until 1982, the last wing to be trained.

Since I retired in 1992 I know the training course length and content has changed as times dictate. Since 1956 there had been a strong military influence again with the classes called wings, parade ground training, "barracks", ranks etc. I understand that this may not now be the case which is sad in a way as there is a tradition here going back to the early styles of policing in colonial New Zealand.

I am pleased that education standards continue to rise but this must not be at the cost of having sensible, sound, very fit, well-balanced young people in the service because policing is about people and the ability to relate to and accept all walks of life and is now harder than ever physically.

Special Branch

Going back to a least the start of the 20th century the New Zealand police always had some sort of intelligence gathering system or group, particularly during the two world wars with the danger of espionage at the forefront of the government's mind. The police were involved in the location and capture or internment of aliens with the military supplying the guards and facilities.

Intelligence gathering is part of any police service worth its salt, particularly in relation to criminals, subversives and political radicals. Up until 1955 the police assumed responsibility for this role, excepting for a short period during the Second World War when this was taken over by the military under the command of a junior British MI5 officer Major Kenneth Folkes.

Folkes appointment was as a result of a request from Britain that an MI5 officer be seconded to head the new Security Intelligence Bureau or SIB. This did not go well, with the Bureau staff distancing themselves from detectives under the control of Detective Sergeant P J (Jim) Nalder. Nalder ran the police intelligence service, such as it was from the late 1930s to the formation of the Security Intelligence Service in 1956, when police got rid of the responsibility of trying to operate a Security Service as well as undertake normal police duties including the gathering of criminal intelligence.

The SIB irritated the police in terms of duplication of inquiries; a slightly superior attitude displayed from the SIB officers towards experienced detectives, these SIB officers being employed off the street but ostensibly of a higher calibre in terms of education and intelligence to police detectives. They also had access to more resources such as vehicles and money.

At that time the SIB was answerable to the military until an embarrassing incident occurred when Folkes was publicly duped by a convicted confidence trickster, S.G Ross, who concocted a hoax about having enemy invasion plans. It was the police who unmasked Ross after he had lived well for some months at the expense of the military authorities. He was arrested in New Plymouth by the police. Folkes was sent back to Britain in embarrassment and the control of the SIB passed to Superintendent James Cummings, the brother of then Commissioner Denis Cummings, answerable to the Prime Minister and the Military Chiefs of Staff. The SIB was quickly disbanded at the cessation of hostilities in September 1945 and all records transferred to the police.

At that point James Cummings had succeeded his brother as Commissioner and intelligence gathering continued although there is little record of security activity by the police from 1945 to 1947. The police was in a shabby and disorganised state after the war with wartime appointed staff rapidly leaving the police and some police who left to join the military rejoining. The service was severely under-manned and overstretched, buildings were in a state of disrepair, the vehicle fleet was old and in need to updating. Wartime austerity meant not much in the way of changes was likely for a while.

Pressure from allies, particularly the USA and the United Kingdom resulted in some Commonwealth countries, including New Zealand, setting up Special Branches following the model of the British Special Branch of the Metropolitan police in London. New Zealand's Special Branch, set up around 1948 would attempt to fulfil in miniature the functions of both the British Special branch and security service, known as MI 5.

It was to fail due to being overloaded with work and partly because police work and security work are incompatible in crucial ways.

The Soviets set up a legation in Wellington towards the end of 1945, a branch office of the Soviet Embassy in Canberra, Australia. It was very heavily staffed compared to the little amount of work required. It was, of course, set up as an intelligence-gathering unit for the Soviet government. The police were totally ill-equipped to monitor or deal with the large influx of spies into Wellington under the guise of drivers, domestic staff and clerks. The New Zealand Government was also kept in the dark by other overseas governments and security services, our allies, because security procedures were considered unacceptably lax in Godzone.

In March 1948 Sir Percy Sillitoe, the director of MI5, made a brief quiet visit to New Zealand. This was prompted by the Malayan emergency and alarm in Victoria about the activities of the Australian Communist Party. While Sillitoe's influence on the development of the New Zealand Special Branch should not be over-estimated his philosophy for the workings of a security service was fully accepted in high government circles and can still be seen in the founding charter of the Security Intelligence Service (SIS).

Records are sparse on Sillitoe's visit but it seems he recommended a security service based within the police if this was considered to be the best option for local practice.

From Sillitoe's visit in 1948 to the setup of the Security Intelligence Service in 1956 the police operated a Special Branch staffed under the direction of Jim Nalder, with a mixture of police and civilian specialists.

The Special Branch was overrun with work when National Conscription was started as the government required full background checks on all young soldiers prior to acceptance for training. By 1956 the workload was out of hand with 6000 requests for assistance received that year. Whilst this was going on Special Branch still had to monitor the movement of known radicals into and out of the country, make security checks on migrants, especially aliens from behind the Iron curtain, meeting every ship and aeroplane from overseas to question passengers. There was very little time to monitor the Soviet's activities. Jim Nalder assumed the rank of Superintendent during his time in Special Branch to reflect the importance of the Special Branch but also to give him sufficient rank to deal with outside agencies and high-ranking military officers.

From 1952 onwards Special Branch continued under the guidance of Commissioner Eric Compton. Telecommunications improved but were still very poor, teleprinters arrived, but the police was, generally in a bad state, resulting in a Commission of Enquiry in 1954, the departure of Compton and the appointment of Sam Barnett as Controller-General in 1956. We will see more about that shortly. At that time the Police shed its role as spy catchers and intelligence gatherers, except for criminal intelligence. A new agency, the New Zealand Security Intelligence Service, began operating in 17th November 1956, completely separate from the police.

From reading the history of firstly the SIB and then the SB war forced the government's hand in terms of setting up a military-run intelligence service but it was poorly set up and badly led, the staff were, whilst some of higher education than the average detective, not as well trained and not as willing to work with experiences detectives as they should have been. Information was not shared willingly, but to be fair this worked both ways apparently.

Most operatives and staff disappeared when the SIB folded. The Special Branch was police-run and employed detectives and specialist civilian staff such as radio experts, they were granted detective rank and paid accordingly, some staying with the police after 1956 and some maybe going to the SIS, but who knows, they are very secretive.

In about 1976 I spent some time working in the police information section at Knigges Avenue, Wellington for a few weeks after upsetting someone for some reason, I cannot recall the details. Much of my day was doing manual checks for the SIS. They still had to access the police Criminal Record Branch for information on subjects. This was before the Whanganui Computer came fully on stream so records were all manual. It kept two of us fully occupied on night shifts between answering teleprinter requests from around the country for police information.

Of course the Criminal Intelligence Section, under way in the 1970s, proved invaluable for serving police. I am sure it still exists nowadays but probably with another name.

Commissioner St John Branigan
Planner for the Civil Policing of New Zealand

New Zealand was a wide open, tough frontier society in the 19th century. The period between 1840 and 1872 was riven with war in the North Island between Maori and British military settler militias. At that time the South Island was the driver of the colony's small economy based on pastoral farming and gold. There was some antipathy directed from the good burghers of the Southern towns towards the North due to what they felt was unscrupulous land-grabbing by various businessmen and speculators, resulting in war, the expense of which was beginning to have to be met from the South Island farmers and business-people.

Along with the rough and ready society was an equally rough and ready policing system, town-based constables or paramilitary type mounted soldier-police. Recruiting standards were not high, neither were standards of literacy and numeracy. Most of the provincial governments paid their police abysmally, usually below an average labourer's daily rate, sometimes as low as four shillings per day, roughly $40NZ per day in present value. Many police had none or few days off, remained in uniform, worked very long hours or split shifts in any one 24 hour period and could be dismissed at the whim of the provincial Superintendent. Illness, alcoholism and early death were common. Apart from the dangers of policing a rough and non-law-abiding male dominated society, dangerous enough as that was, there was also the added risks of just living in a frontier society, riding accidents and drownings took their toll on the populace, police included.

Police were heavily armed until almost the formation of the present police in 1886. From then forward arms were always available if needed but not generally carried, society requiring a somewhat less coercive police model by then.

When considering early policing in New Zealand one has to take the above into account when looking at the "models" of policing adopted. A version of the English "bobby" system was used in the larger towns with beats and shifts. However most of the country needed a coercive, heavily armed and mostly mounted police service.

This was based on the paramilitary Irish Constabulary model copied in Victoria from Ireland in the 1850's and in Canada with the formation of the North West Mounted Police in the late 1870s. Constables were virtually soldiers, they lived in barracks or camps, they were moved around the country constantly to stop fraternisation difficulties and many were as rough, drunken and morally corrupt as most of their clients. They were led by military trained officers and senior NCOs and were subject to a form of martial law. This saw many police gaoled for disciplinary offences by their own. I am not sure whether or not they remained in the police after discharge from prison, maybe, maybe not, depending on the offence I guess.

Things were getting a bit difficult in Otago in about 1861with gold fields attracting miners from around the world with associated lawlessness, increased crime but huge profits. The Superintendent of Otago Province, J L C Richardson, decided he needed an Irish Constabulary style police force for the gold fields and gold escort duties. He decided to import a few experienced and senior police from Victoria, a colony well-versed in such policing of unruly miners and associates; bar managers, gamblers, conmen, thieves and prostitutes. The canny Scottish settlers of Otago, a very strait-laced bunch, did not approve of the shenanigans of this motley lot but also did not mind the huge wealth the gold mines produced in Dunedin.

Enter the man who was to become the father of New Zealand policing in the 19th century, St John Branigan. I am not sure how his first name is pronounced but it could be "SinJin", an upper class affectation from jolly old England.

Branigan was born in about 1824 into a humble Catholic family in King's County, Ireland. He joined the 45th (1st Nottinghamshire Regiment, which was sent to Cape Colony, South Africa in 1845. Branigan was an ambitious and very able individual. Anticipating quicker advancement he left the army and joined the Cape Police, seeing active service during frontier warfare. He was wounded and decorated for gallantry. At five foot 8 inches he was short for a police officer but his efficiency ensured rapid promotion to Inspector. In 1851 he married Margaret Hudd.

In 1853, with a view to a fast buck, he spent all his savings on a schooner of merchandise, left the police and sailed to Melbourne with the intention of selling the merchandise on the goldfields. Things did not work out and he found himself in the Victoria Police in 1854. Victoria had to form a police service based on the paramilitary policing modes of the London Metropolitan Police and the Irish Constabulary. By 1856 Branigan had achieved the rank of Sub-Inspector. Branigan was apparently, by nature, a difficult and forceful personality to manage but admired and recognised for his other qualities as a police officer.

Coincidentally, and thankfully for New Zealand, the Victorian Police was going through a retrenchment at the time of Superintendent Richardson's request for some ranking Victorian Police to come to New Zealand to form a new, paramilitary type force with emphasis on policing the goldfields. Branigan was the most junior commissioned officer in the police and faced no secure future. The Chief Commissioner of the Victorian Police Frederick Standish, took the opportunity to rid himself of "one of our best and most efficient officers" but also a pain in his posterior, sounds familiar. Transfer the problem child, always a good Human Resource tactic.

Branigan, his family and a few other Victorian Police arrived in Dunedin in August 1861. He received so much latitude in forming his new police that half the provincial expenditure was going into the establishment of the new force.

Branigan brought a sense of professionalism to policing in the Otago Province. Specialist aspects of policing were introduced for the first time in the colony, detection, preventive policing patrols (beats), part-time employment of female searchers, a water police and the publication of the first Police Gazette. Branigan was a martinet on supervision. Surprising staff at unexpected visits to police stations to ensure their degree of efficiency; he embarked on strenuous tours of inspection haunted the docks for recruits among new immigrants and reported daily to his political masters. By April 1862 he had increased the force to 100, by far the largest police force in the colony. Shortly after he was allowed to double this to 200 in late 1862 due to the increasing need for policing in the goldfield districts. Within a year his fame had become legendary, his force was popularly known as "'Branigan's Troopers", universally admitted to be the best police force, not only in the colonies, but in the World!!!

He had a town named after him St Johns, later changed to Kingston. He mixed easily with the great and good of Otago, enjoying influence at high levels in society. He was single-minded in the pursuit of justice, even charging a miner with murder despite witnesses providing a water-tight alibi for the guy at the loer court hearing. Only when Queenstown's resident magistrate, John Wood, testified that the defendant had been serving on his coroner's jury at the time of the murder was the accused, bankrupted and broken in health by then, set free. Wood later recalled that Branigan's prey had been taken from him. Branigan never spoke to the magistrate again.

Branigan liked to gild the lily a bit for his political masters, over-playing the presence of Australian criminals in the province a bit too much, trying to ensure his budget remained generous. With gold mining quietening down the force was reduced to below 100 by the end of 1867, still the most formidable force in New Zealand.

In 1867 the General Government had formed the Armed Constabulary, a force to deal with insurrectionist Maori in the North Island. In 1868, with the withdrawal of the British Army regiments, it quickly evolved into a military force. By June 1869 the rebellions had almost died out, except for Titokowaru and Te Kooti. Branigan was brought to Wellington to advise on how to de-militarise the Armed Constabulary. His long-term plan transitioning to a civilian policing model nationally so impressed Premier Fox and Defence Secretary Donald McLean that they asked him to implement it personally.

As Commissioner of the Armed Constabulary he threw his "boundless energy" into converting an army of "ragged and war-torn soldiers" into a highly trained force of police. He started the first training depot in Wellington at Mt Cook and men of "good education and good position" were soon replacing the many hundreds of discharged unsuitable Armed Constabulary staff. He brought J B Thomson, his Chief Detective in Otago, to Wellington to set up a North Island detection service with concentration on illegal arms trading with Maori.

Turning soldiers into police made Branigan many influential enemies in the provinces. Te Kooti was still causing trouble on the East Coast but this was solved by using Kupapa or Maori forces led by European officers to chase Te Kooti and his gang out of the Urewera and into exile in the King Country, killing many of his group in the process.

By the end of 1869 the Armed Constabulary had been halved to 1000 men but continuing opposition to demilitarisation from both within and outside the force, adverse publicity, and the physical hardship of travel to remote outposts all greatly affected Branigan's mental health. Never the easiest of chappies to work with at the best of times his irritable, quarrelsome and autocratic nature now intensified. He was trying to turn the Auckland City Police into part of the national force and this was being resisted by the Auckland provincial councillors who, for their own reasons, wanted to keep their own police. Late in January 1871 Branigan suffered "sunstroke" at Onehunga. He began attacking people and was locked up in the Auckland Lunatic Asylum. A transfer back to Wellington on full pay did not help and he was described as "mad as a hatter". In May 1871 he was committed to the Dunedin Asylum under the Lunacy Act and a successor as Commissioner appointed. From April 1872 he was under constant and severe restraint (straitjacket). He died on 11 September 1873 from "softening of the brain". A 24 foot high monument was constructed in Dunedin to his memory.

Branigan was the most influential policing figure in the 19th century in New Zealand, providing in less than ten years precisely the type of policing organisation needed in the colony. His fame and his system transcended his end.

In 1876 provincial governments were abolished in New Zealand and the Armed Constabulary absorbed the provincial police forces to become the colony's only police. Once this merger was completed, in 1877, it was renamed the New Zealand Constabulary Force with two main divisions, the Policing Branch and the Reserve Division, later the Field Force.

By the mid-1880s the colonial frontier was considered to have been tamed to the extent that its policing and military functions could be formally separated. In 1886 the civil constables became the New Zealand Police Force and the Reserve Force of military constables became the Field Force. This was all down to St John

Branigan's long term plan, honoured in its execution by his successors following his early death at about 50.

Commissioner John Cullen
First Commissioner to rise from the rank of Constable in New Zealand

Up until the early years of the 20th century New Zealand was a wide open, often lawless, frontier society, especially in the North Island. Firearms formed part of everyday life for civilians, police and soldiers alike, Maori and Pakeha. The American Wild West has been glorified on film and in literature but the "wild west" of frontier New Zealand was probably as awful, violent and deadly at times. Death was a constant companion for early settler and Maori due to the simple act of trying to survive in a hostile environment together with the depredations of criminals and warring Iwi.

Policing such a society, dating back to the 1850s when the country was beginning to be settled by the thousands, mainly from the United Kingdom and the other Australasian colonies required a system that was para-military and at the coercive end of the scale of law enforcement. Mounted and armed police existed in country areas with armed foot police in towns and villages.

The Gold Rush of the 1850s in Otago saw lawlessness reach its height in the South Island, then the economic power house of New Zealand. The North Island at the time was still mostly untamed hostile territory.

We have already seen the influence of St John Branigan and his Otago Police on the transition to and development of a national police service beginning in 1886, moving from a coercive Armed Constabulary based on the Irish and Victoria Constabulary models to the more benign model of policing developed in Victorian England. In 1876, the last year of the New Zealand Armed Constabulary, John Cullen, ex Royal Irish Constabulary, arrived in New Zealand and joined the Armed Constabulary.

Cullen was born in Glenfarne, County Leitrim, Ireland on 28 March 1850. He received a modest education, leaving school before the completion of his primary education to work on his parents' small leased holding. This was a time of turmoil in Ireland with insurrection in the air, criminal gangs active throughout rural Ireland and poverty following the potato famine. Ireland was emptying out, Irish leaving for all points of the compass for a better life. Cullen grew up seeing the Irish Constabulary, later Royal Irish Constabulary, active in controlling by coercive force a population down-trodden but in rebellion. The RIC was basically an Irish military force and acted in the interests of the Crown and landowners.

As the third son in his family Cullen had little prospects of working his parents holding, land owned by Arthur Tottenham of nearby Glenfarne Hall. In 1869, at the age of 19 he enlisted in the RIC as a sub Constable and was stationed in barracks well away from his home. Cullen, with his physical fitness, staring eyes and rigid stance, took well to this form of policing. Life was harsh in the RIC and men were not permitted to marry until they had served seven years, living in barracks with frequent transfers until marriage. Cullen proved to be an exceptional policeman and in 1874, less than five years into his very long policing career, he married Rachel McGinley, an early privilege accorded to few young single Constables who were showing exceptional promise.

Promotion was stifled for any ambitious RIC officer, of which Cullen was one, as all Commissioned Officers were a class apart from the men they commanded. Also the main body of the RIC was 75% Catholic while the Officer Corps was 80% Protestant. This led to severe dissatisfaction for many, resulting in many RIC members leaving for other police services in the colonies or the USA.

In March 1876 Cullen resigned his post with the RIC and he, Rachel and children embarked on the Camperdown, bound for New Zealand. On the voyage Cullen was one of three male passengers appointed Constables to control the passengers.

Upon arrival in New Zealand, in July 1876 Cullen joined the New Zealand Armed Constabulary. He was the first person to graduate from the Armed Constabulary depot into the police branch of the unified New Zealand Constabulary Force then being established.

Promotion came quick for Cullen, impressing his superiors with his stature, appearance, zeal and tough attitude. He was posted to Blenheim in January 1877, being promoted to Sergeant in July 1878. He soon obtained a reputation as a strict disciplinarian and survived a number of complaints of overbearing conduct towards his men and towards the public. He moved through the then three classes of NCO, serving in Dunedin, Timaru, Christchurch, Napier as sub-district commander from 1891 and Whanganui.

One of the biggest issues bedevilling the Police in the late 19th and early 20th centuries was the issue of sly-grog dens. Temperance movements abounded in New Zealand and came very close to obtaining full prohibition throughout the country during several elections between 1911 and 1987.

In 1897 Cullen was disguised as an insurance agent and sent on a special undercover assignment into the King Country, then dry, to entrap sly-grog sellers, securing the convictions of 26 prominent violators of the licensing laws and much praise from authorities harried by temperance campaigners.

Later that year, in September, Cullen achieved the impossible for an RIC member in Ireland, he was promoted to the position of Inspector third class and was posted to Greymouth, in charge of the

Nelson and Westland police district. In 1898 he was sent to relieve as district commander for Auckland, Waikato, the Bay of Islands and other northern areas, the position made permanent in December 1898.

Cullen was a strict disciplinarian, acknowledging "I am naturally a strict man". Two Commissioners, John Tunbridge and his successor Walter Dinnie at the time needed a tough Inspector in the Auckland area due to "a state of great disorganisation" at the time. Serious shortcomings had arisen in terms of supervision, the ability of sick and old NCOs and a poor performance in terms of general policing arising out of a Royal Commission of Inquiry at the time in which Cullen gave extensive evidence. The Commissioners were prepared to overlook serious indiscretions made by Cullen which included open feuds with subordinates and important local public figures and his vindictiveness towards many he had fallen out with. Cullen kept tight control over his men through a system of espionage run by his favourites within the Auckland district police and by civilian observers. It was a popularly held belief that "Czar Cullen" went beyond strictness and into the realms of the unscrupulous when dealing with police staff.

Cullen expected to be made Commissioner after the retirement of Tunbridge and was again disappointed when Dinnie was forced to resign at the end of 1909 after yet another commission of inquiry. The Under Secretary of Justice at the time, Frank Waldegrave, took over the running of the police as a civilian from 1909 to late 1912. Cullen blamed his missing out on the Commissionership on anti-Catholic influence. Back then sectarian feeling still ran very high. A goodly proportion of the police were Catholic due to the number of Irish immigrants who became police in the late 19th and early 20th century. These sectarian feelings run right through the history of the police, well into the 20th century, not openly and provably stated but always implied. Where the truth is may be difficult to resolve. Cullen was Catholic and it is known that there was a strong anti-Catholic movement in New Zealand at the time trying to influence government.

Cullen liked to cultivate friendships among the great and good in New Zealand, regarding those below his station in life with mostly contempt unless they were of use to him. He became a favourite of the leader of the Reform Party, William Massey and another Reform politician Alexander Herdman. Upon the Reform Party coming into power in 1912 Massey became Prime Minister and Herdman became Minister of Police. Upon Waldegrave's retirement the short lived Liberal government of Thomas McKenzie had appointed Cullen Commissioner in April 1912 despite "determined, if not diabolical" opposition to him.

This made John Cullen the first New Zealand Police Commissioner to rise from the ranks.

The Reform Party gave Cullen carte blanche to deal with ongoing industrial unrest at the Waihi gold mine.

Cullen liked to be "on the ground" rather than trusting his senior officers to run operations. Three major operations, an insurrection by a local Maori chief Kuao in Kaikohe over possession of firearms, the mine strike at Waihi and the Kenana debacle in 1916 were all examples of Cullen's hands on and very aggressive approach to issues of the day surrounding Maori wish for independence and industrial unrest.

The Waihi town was normally a very peaceful small country town with a prosperous gold mine. When industrial unrest caused a strike at the mine Cullen flooded the town with 70 armed police, taking personal command of the situation and supporting strike-breakers to ensure the mine continued to operate. Massey's Reform government was implacably opposed to any unionism amongst the working classes and gave Cullen carte blanche to do what needed to be done. This resulted in a police encouraged and sanctioned attack on the Unionists hall in Waihi, leading to the death of a striker, Fred Evans. One of Cullen's strengths was his management of media, way ahead of his time. This resulted in news not being as open and as forthright as would be expected nowadays. The Waihi strike rolled to its end, the miners and their families being forced out of town and the mine staffed by strike-breakers and others.

The episode concerning Rua Kenana is well outlined in an earlier chapter and shows Cullen in terrible light, arranging perjured evidence, implication in the killing and possible murder of two men, jury-rigging, the use of influence to sway a Judge, bullying of defence counsel and under-mining the Crown Prosecutor are some of the sins that are now laid at his feet. He also caused many serving police involved in the affair disquiet. Some left, some were transferred into ignominy, others felt pressured to give perjured evidence, refusing and having their careers ended or blighted going forward.

Cullen was, by today's standards, an autocratic and difficult leader who could not delegate to or trust his senior officers. He was also a very able and ruthless policeman, perhaps needed at a time when the New Zealand police was finding its feet after a series of Royal Commissions of Inquiry showed deficiencies in leadership, supervision recruitment and training. He was the first New Zealand police officer to become Commissioner, rising from the rank of Constable. It would be another 10 years after his tenure ended before the first New Zealand born Commissioner, William McIlveney, was appointed in 1926.

Cullen retired from the police not long after the Kenana affair, late in 1916, with war still raging. He continued to work in public office, being appointed Commissioner of Aliens in the Defence Department. He found compulsory employment for and supervised enemy aliens, mostly Dalmatian gum-diggers, paying at piece –rates. When this was objected to by the workers he labelled them shirkers and Bolsheviks, interning or gaoling the offenders and threatening to expel them from New Zealand.

He left this position in 1919 and retired to follow his interest in conservation work in the National Park area, wanting to introduce exotic animals from the UK for sporting purposes. This plan was unsuccessful but he did manage to introduce the heather that now is prolific in the area, at the expense of native flora.

He was a complex man who died in 1939.

I feel that Cullen was unusual in one other aspect, he trained in the Royal Irish Constabulary but upon arriving in New Zealand he joined the New Zealand Armed Constabulary, transferred to the police branch of the New Zealand Constabulary force in 1877 and then in 1886 transferred to the New Zealand Police Force, serving in all three national police services in New Zealand. He policed from wild and woolly frontier times where war was till a strong possibility through to modern 20th century New Zealand.

He was also the Commissioner who stymied the first attempt to start a Police Association in 1913. That is a later story.

Commissioner John "Bruce" Young
From Police Industrial Advocate to Commissioner

Since the early days of policing in New Zealand there have been many Commissioners, firstly military-trained officers and then, from the late 19th century Commissioners selected from the police itself. Many have been outstanding men, no women yet. One or two were not good, one bordering on the criminal. Most have been good holders of the office for their time. I have written about New Zealand's only civilian Controller-General Samuel Barnett, lawyer and public administrator, the person I regard as the father of the modern New Zealand police service, giving senior police the opportunity to grow and develop the service in the late 1950s after the short and controversial reign of Commissioner Eric Compton. Barnett, whilst the third civilian Controller-General of police, was succeeded by Willis Spencer Brown, a serving senior police officer, as Controller-General until the passage of the 1958 Police Act after which Brown became Commissioner of Police.

There have been two further times in the history of the modern police where civilians have headed the police, Frank Waldegrave from December 1909 to 1912, also serving as Under-Secretary of Justice, after Commissioner Walter Dinnie's term as Commissioner ended suddenly and then again for a month Robert Percy Ward, again Under-Secretary of Justice, headed the police after Commissioner William McIlveney, the first New Zealand-born Commissioner, left the office in 1930. Like Compton, but for differing reasons, the departures of Dinnie and McIlveney were unusual.

I have also written about military and Victoria Police trained Commissioner St John Branigan whose plan presented to the Fox ministry in 1869 began the transition from a military style coercive policing model based on the Irish Constabulary to the more benign model adopted from 1886. Branigan died very young in an asylum and did not see his plan through but successive Commissioners did.

In my research travels I come across many interesting stories of yester-year and of men who made a difference either to their colleagues' lot or to policing itself.

One of these men was John Bruce Young, known as Bruce. He was born in Kaiapoi on 25 August 1888 to farming parents and was educated to Standard six level (year eight) before leaving school in 1902 to drive a storekeeper's cart. Looking for a bigger challenge, he began a bakery apprenticeship in Kaiapoi, then working for a baker at Waikari, some 52 kms away from 1905.

In 1909 he returned to work on the family farm after a brother became ill, within six months applying for the New Zealand Police.

Bruce trained at the Wellington South Police Depot and was posted to Auckland at the end of ten weeks training on 1 August 1910 for beat duty in the inner city and later at Ponsonby. Bruce was a conscientious copper, shorter than average, and was soon making his mark locking up bookmakers and ship deserters.

He married Olive Grimwood in 1912 and transferred to the Auckland Detective Office two years later, being appointed Detective in December 1918.

Bruce was ambitious and able, despite his modest education, a normal education for a boy of his class in those days. Universal secondary education did not start in New Zealand until the mid 20th century. In 1919 he was the youngest candidate to pass his Sub-inspector exams, still a Detective.

In May 1920 he helped later Commissioner, but then Detective Sergeant James Cummings to secure the conviction of Dennis Gunn, the first New Zealand murderer to be hanged mostly on fingerprint evidence. Later that year Bruce became the sole Detective at Greymouth.

While serving in Greymouth Bruce investigated a theft by servant complaint at a drapery. The suspect being one Thomas Christopher, ex-Constable late from Timaru, the last person, other than the shooter, to see Constable James Dorgan, before James was shot to death on the beat. Gossip, scuttlebutt and family rumour had laid the blame for the shooting at one stage at Christopher's feet. This was not true. Christopher was with other people when the shots were heard and Dorgan did not mention him as the offender prior to dying shortly afterwards. However the belief by Christopher that he could have been shot instead of Dorgan led him to resign. Over the years there has also been rumour that police in Timaru were involved in commercial burglaries prior to Dorgan's murder. An interesting aside, maybe giving this belief some credence, is the Christchurch-based homicide inquiry team requiring alibis from all serving police in Timaru at the time of the murder.

Christopher moved to Greymouth after leaving the police, working in the drapery store until 1925 when Bruce began his inquiry.

Bruce caught Thomas Christopher red-handed passing four dozen pairs of towels to a member of a rival drapery firm. A subsequent search of Christopher's lodgings found further stolen property and a .45 cal. Webley revolver which he admitted to owning when in the police in Timaru. James was shot with a .32 cal. bullet, probably from a S&W revolver.

On hearing of the arrest Commissioner Arthur H Wright ordered that the Dorgan homicide be re-opened with a view to having Christopher charged with Dorgan's murder. This was quickly put right with the statements taken at the time from the three bystanders with Christopher when the shots were heard from the direction of the store.

Olive Young died in April 1921 leaving Bruce to care for four children aged between eight years and two months. In 1923 Bruce married Olive's widowed cousin Ella Bradshaw, a postmistress from Manakau with two children. They went on to have another two children.

By the time Bruce was dealing with Thomas Christopher he was a Detective Sergeant, transferring to Christchurch shortly after. Bruce was a methodical and taxing investigator. In 1927 he got an accelerated increment in pay due to "exceptional zeal and ability" in prosecuting bookmakers, notably Alfred Whitta who had 3000 clients.

Apart from being a focused and relentless career detective Bruce was also a supporter of police unionism, a member of the first and very short-lived New Zealand Police Association launched in April 1913 and later served as Auckland secretary of the police branch of the PSA. That he attained the highest rank in the police after his early involvement in a doomed police union says a lot for Bruce's ability. Careers were ended or badly dented for some of those involved in the 1913 attempt at forming a Police Association. The Massey government had no time for unions of any stripe.

In August 1936 Bruce chaired the first conference of delegates which secured the approval of Peter Fraser, police minister for the formation of the second New Zealand Police Association. Being stationed in Dunedin at the time prevented Bruce being appointed the first President of the Police Association, all the management committee being based in Wellington. Bill Murray was the first President. Two years later, in 1938, Bruce transferred to

Wellington and Bill happily vacated the president's role for Bruce. Bruce supported the increasingly vigorous advocacy of Jack Meltzer while at the same time containing rank and file restlessness at lack of real progress in industrial matters during war-time. Relations between Commissioner Denis Cummings and the Association; in particular, Jack Meltzer, during 1943 and 1944, were not good, with Cummings only agreeing to communicate with Bruce on Association matters.

As is clear, Bruce was a dedicated and highly competent investigator. He was involved in his share of homicide inquiries during his career, two of which I will mention here; the murder of two Salvation Army women, sisters Annie and Rosamund Smyth in Wairoa in 1942 and another murder, six years later in 1948 in Wairoa, three miles from the Smyth murders, of retired railway worker Herbert William Brunton. Bruce was the officer in charge of both homicide inquiries. Both remain unsolved to this day despite intense and dedicated work by large inquiry teams. Many detectives, at some stage in their careers, have a whodunnit which remains unsolved, few probably have two, linked by location and similar MO. There appeared no motive for the murders, robbery being discounted in the deaths of the sisters as they both had money in their handbags, one a substantial amount for the time, 18 pounds, ($1300 in 2020). Certain similarities pointed to the possibility of the offender being the same in both incidents.

Wellington lawyer George Joseph, in his book "By A Person or Persons Unknown" goes into each case in some detail. He also describes being retained to defend, in 1950, Leo Sylvester Hannan, on a charge of murder, the allegation being that he murdered a railway caretaker who disturbed him during a burglary, the weapon being a heavy spanner. All the Wairoa victims died from severe injuries inflicted by heavy objects. Joseph got on well with Hannan. who was subsequently sentenced to life imprisonment for the murder of the caretaker. Hannan was an experienced criminal in his late forties who had extensive previous convictions for dishonesty and violence. Hannan was diagnosed with terminal cancer and chose to die in prison instead of hospital. He was by then five years into his life term. Joseph visited him, a dying man, being interviewed by his lawyer. Hannan admitted to Joseph he committed the murders of both sisters and, six years later Brunton, for money but found none, just a half bottle of gin at Brunton's bach. He died three months later. Joseph discussed his conversation with pathologist Dr Lynch who undertook the Wairoa sisters' post mortems and the post mortem of the caretaker in the latest murder. Lynch gave evidence that the offender was left-handed. Hannan was left-handed. Interesting. Sherwood Young, Bruce's grandson, learnt the identity of Hannan from Joseph after Hannan's death and, having served in the CIB and being an historian, did his groundwork via the New Zealand Police Gazettes of the years 1942 and 1948, showing Hannan was not in prison at the time of the murders, between prison sentences each time.

In April 1943, 24 years after qualifying for commissioned officer rank, Bruce was promoted to Sub-inspector in charge of detectives in Christchurch. This promotion meant he was required to leave the Police Association, in those days membership being only open to members of police up to and including Senior Sergeant or Chief Detective. From 1943 Bruce rose through the commissioned ranks at some speed and with five more transfers, until his appointment as Commissioner of Police on 4 April 1950.

Bruce inherited a tired, war-weary, and out of date organization with insufficient staff, inadequate facilities and working conditions falling behind those in the community. He also inherited a lack-lustre Minister of Police WH Fortune who would go on to appoint an elder in his church as Bruce's successor after his untimely death, Eric Compton, before being shoved out of the minister-ship and then voted out of parliament in 1954.

Bruce struggled to improve facilities due to Fortune having little influence in cabinet but he did have small and lasting successes. A recruiting campaign bolstered numbers and he introduced open-necked tunics for Constables and put women police into uniform, 11 years after their introduction into the police. He enjoyed a more cordial relationship with the Police Association than his predecessors did as well.

Bruce was then faced with the responsibility for the policing of the 151 day waterfront lockout which crippled New Zealand in 1951. Under his watch the police were very low-key and rarely enforced the emergency regulations. Bruce was at heart a working man so he would have understood the need to police the community with a velvet glove. There was little violence and no special constables were deployed in public as happened in 1890, 1913 and 1932. There was, however, a Civil Emergency Organisation of several thousand men around New Zealand, plainclothes volunteers who patrolled city streets unobtrusively, each Mayor being responsible for their local group.

The dispute, combined with lack of government support, took its toll on Bruce in terms of his health, as it did quite a few other senior police. It is said that the post war period, culminating in the waterfront dispute shortened the lives of many senior police and resulting in a real lack of depth at high levels in the police in the early to mid-1950s.

In 1952 Bruce's health worsened and he died in Wellington on 28 December 1952, with Eric Compton appointed straight from being the most junior Sub-inspector to Assistant Commissioner, in control of the police while Bruce was ill. When told of the appointment by the Police Minister, Bruce is said to have replied "over my dead body". He had planned for Superintendent Cornelius Murphy of Christchurch to replace him but, unfortunately ill, Murphy died on 26 January 1953, within a month of his own death.

Why do I think this Commissioner was different? He had a strong industrial advocacy background at a time when this was not welcome by government, employers or farmers, he was the key figure behind the formation of the New Zealand Police Association and then went on to become Commissioner. His Commissionership was, in some ways, a poisoned chalice. He inherited a hapless Minister in a National government, a party not known for its love of unions; a broken and possibly also slightly bent police service; a tired and possibly ill top administration; recruiting issues and the largest industrial dispute in New Zealand's history. That he managed this potentially disastrous event with little fuss and with the police reputation as enforcers essentially intact is, I believe, a credit to a man of humble origins and modest education, but who had a deep concern for the hard-pressed staff he led. The tributes of many organisations and individuals when he died being testament to this fact.

In writing this article I sought the advice of Chief Inspector (Retired) Sherwood Young MA(Hons), MBE, police historian, Bruce's grandson. I would like to thank Sherwood for his kind guidance, collaboration and support. In our communications Sherwood made the following comment, best left in his own words:
"On analysis, I think my grandfather was terribly unfortunate, in so many ways. Consider that his first born was a polio (infantile paralysis) sufferer who remained at home throughout Bruce's life; his older brother was killed at war and his son who was named after his dead brother died as a young child; his wife died aged 33; he was required to transfer ten times during his 42 year career; as Commissioner he was faced with 151 days of a nationwide industrial dispute; he died aged only 64 being unable to retire; he had no house and his widow was given three weeks to quit her home by a successor he did not want. I feel a great deal of compassion for him."

Commissioner Eric Compton
A Crisis in Policing 1950 to 1955

This is the a tale of a 5 year period in the New Zealand Police that resulted in the foundations of policing that we all know today in New Zealand. It started with the appointment of a highly respected Commissioner who died in office, leading to the appointment of a highly unpopular Commissioner who leap-frogged over two ranks to be appointed by the then Minister of Police having only been commissioned a short time as a Sub inspector, leading to another Royal Commission of Inquiry into the Police. The Inquiry looked at several areas including the following, telephone tapping by the Commissioner when a detective and later allegedly when a Commissioner, allegations of bribery of Police by bookmakers, allegations that the Police were not enforcing the licensing regulations, employment of police with criminal records and private work being done at police expense on the Commissioner's privately owned home. It was later found that 54 members of the police had non-traffic convictions ranging from liquor-related offences to rape.

There were also other allegations floating around including an effort to break the domination of the police Officer Corps by Freemason and Catholics, police regularly receiving "brown paper bags" containing cash to turn a blind eye to the activities of bookies, promotion based on merit for three sergeants direct to Inspector, skipping the rank of Senior Sergeant, for specialist roles. All were subsequently returned to Sergeants but later went on to have great careers in high rank.

In February 1950 John "Bruce" Young was appointed Commissioner, taking over a Police "Force" of around 1600 men and women. He had as an officer corps between 5 and 7 superintendents, about 18 inspectors and about 12 sub inspectors, a rank that was to disappear after the Commission of Inquiry. There were no Assistant or Deputy Commissioner and no Chief Superintendents, a reasonably flat command structure.

Following World War 2 many of the senior officers were old and ill, facing retirement. Commissioner Young came in with great promise, respected by all staff. He had helped to set up the Police Association and was considered more in touch with the man on the beat than most of his predecessors. He tried to advance radio technology but was thwarted by the recently appointed National government who did not like spending money on public services.

Commissioner Young is best remembered for the careful and diplomatic way he handled the 1951 Waterfront Lockout. Special regulations were put in place that were draconian, to say the least, but Young ensured that some humanity was included in the enforcement by police. In fact most of the regulations were simply not enforced. Young's strong union sympathies, shared by many of his staff, probably saved the country from a lot of violence and disorder.

All staff leave and days off were cancelled for the 151 days of the strike and this, with the huge responsibility of ensuring peace was maintained, is suspected to have contributed to the early deaths of many senior police, including Young.

Young's successor prior to and following his death was Eric Compton, appointed in December 1952. He was not Young's choice of successor, very much not. Compton had only been a sub inspector for some months after promotion from chief detective. By all accounts he was not a popular fellow with peers or staff, certainly not with senior officers.

Compton was an elder of the Plymouth Brethren and the then Minister of Police, WH Fortune, was a junior member of his congregation. Fortune was a lacklustre MP who eventually got the boot from the police portfolio and then from parliament. Fortune promoted Compton over the heads of senior sub inspectors, all inspectors and all superintendents. At the time there was police lore that the higher command of the police was dominated by Freemasons and Catholics and a reason put forward for Compton's appointment was to break this tradition.

As an aside this lore was still around when I arrived at Lower Hutt in 1971. When a couple of older cops found out I was Catholic I was told not to bother to apply for the CIB in the Hutt as it was all masons, but do not worry because the Staff Senior Sergeant and at least one of the Uniform Branch Senior Sergeants were Catholics so I will be alright. I was a bit bemused by this and took it as a joke, ending up in the CIB within a few years anyway with a whole lot of other Catholics. No idea about the Masons as they were not open about their membership of course. Good gossip anyway, who knows how truthful it was.

It was alleged that Compton was eavesdropping on staff by telephone, getting private work done at Police expense, had no time whatsoever for policewomen, had a radio installed at his own home to listen in on the patrol cars in Wellington, hoping to catch staff out and wanting to put in place a merit based promotion system, anathema to the Police Association in those days.

I do recall old cops from those days talking about Compton as being a crook and as Police National HQ in Johnson Street being a den of sexual misbehaviour, all very scandalous to my very young ears. Like the Catholic/Mason thing, maybe some small substance in fact but a good story nevertheless.

The inquiry resulted in Compton and two other senior officers being unable to really explain why they had large sums of money in their possession, Compton's at his home and one other

officer in his locker. Both claimed rigorous thrift, and on Compton's behalf, selling eggs and auction goods and on the other officer's behalf successful horse racing. The sums were in the vicinity of £2,000 each, a small fortune in those days, ($109,000 NZ in 2020)..
Certainly not sums that serving police could easily explain and more than the annual salary of both men.

It seems that a lot went on that did not make it into the newspapers of the time or into accessible files. Despite the suspicions the Commission cleared Compton and the other two officers of wrongdoing. This was not the end of matters for Compton. At the first national meeting of Commissioned Officers for three years in January 1955 Superintendent John Edwards moved a motion of no confidence in the Commissioner but this failed. The following day Prime Minster Holland arrived to address the conference. The officers then protested their loyalty to the government but pointed out that the recent Commission of Inquiry lacked legal validity and that its findings could be overturned in Court. Holland spoke to the conference for 90 minutes. What was discussed is not known but he managed to change the vote of no confidence in the Commissioner to a vote of confidence in the Commission. He went overseas after the conference and it was widely rumoured he was calling on Scotland Yard in the hope of getting a new Commissioner.

The Commission of Inquiry limped on for another 3 months, wracked by squabbling and controversy until 20 April 1955 when Compton "retired". He managed to get a fairly hefty package as a farewell present. He managed to get £6000 compensation for loss of contract, superannuation of 812 pound per year and six months retiring leave. A new word was introduced to Police jargon "Comptonsation".

The rest is history and, to do it justice, needs to be a separate story, the appointment of ST Barnett as Controller-General of Police and the huge reforms that this great man introduced, modernising the police completely.

Controller-General Samuel Barnett
The founder of a modern Police Department 1955 - 1958

Samuel Thompson Barnett was born to a working class family in Dunedin in 1901. He was a trained solicitor, initially joining the Department of Lands and survey, later becoming the first superintendent of staff training in the public service. He later became Assistant Director of Education, appointed Under Secretary for Justice in 1949 before taking up a Carnegie Fellowship, travelling to Great Britain and the United States of America to study penal and criminological developments. During his trip he observed British and American police services and was eventually appointed to the International Committee set up by the United Nations to investigate the prevention and treatment of crime.

The Minister of Police who appointed Commissioner Compton, WH Fortune, was eventually sacked from his portfolio, later leaving parliament. Due to the ructions caused by Compton and the subsequent Commission of Inquiry the Police Ministership was handled by the Prime Minister, Sid Holland. The Police was regarded as a department out of its time, badly led, poorly manned and in need of modernising in all areas.

When Holland travelled overseas in 1955 it was rumoured he was head-hunting a new Commissioner capable of modernising the service but who had no ties to the past. After Compton's "retirement" it was clear that there were few senior serving officers with the ability, education and foresight to be truly innovative, hence the possible need for an "outsider". Holland was determined not to have a repeat of the Compton debacle, appointing a junior officer not fitted to the role. The two most senior officers, Peter Munroe of Auckland and Denis Sugrue of Christchurch both declined the appointment, probably with good reason. Other senior officers were regarded as too close to retirement.

The government was determined to modernise the police and to have, as its head, whoever was needed to do this. Holland appointed Sam Barnett as clearly the most talented and educated public administrator available. He was Secretary for Justice at the time, a role he maintained as well as Controller-General of the Police. A full day's work. Barnett was not sworn but was entitled to be uniformed. He chose not to as this would be logistically difficult in terms of his two roles. He also felt it was an inappropriate idea anyway.

Barnett was also a keen observer and communicator with police on the street. He liked a whisky or three and would often come out on late shifts to observe what was happening with a certain redolence about him. He could be very short with some but came to be liked and respected by the rank and file. He had a big job on his hands with a three year definite term, it being the Prime Minister's intention to later appoint another New Zealand officer as Commissioner of Police.

Barnett set about appointing some of the country's most talented people to police senior roles in public relations, administrative reform, education and training, statistics, health and personnel. He also recognised the need to upgrade the educational grunt of the average cop on the street. At the time education levels were very low with just the requirement to have a standard six, Year eight, education. Recruiting was a mixed bag until the mid-1950s with trainers commenting that some recruits arriving simply did not have the literary and numeracy skills to cope with basic police work, could not speak confidently, some with serious intellectual deficiencies. I guess these people struggled, some surviving somehow but most moving on.

From 1955 training and recruitment policies were introduced

that saw the educational level of recruits lift to at least fourth form level, going higher later. The rank system was also attacked. The role of Sub-Inspector was abolished with Chief Inspector and Chief Superintendent being added. Promotion by merit was started instead of solely by seniority, a change fought desperately by the New Zealand Police Association. This took some time to bed in and become accepted, the Association doing its members no real favours in the long term with its initial stance. Promotion by seniority, or serious lack of, was a hit and miss affair at the best of times with consequences just witnessed in the Compton affair.

Barnett set in place a major building programme for police houses and new police stations throughout New Zealand, he greatly expanded the vehicle fleet but was frustrated with the lack of choice the Police had in models. He had virtually an open purse from the government to bring the police into the mid-20th century and out of the 19th century.

Commissioner Young had introduced the open neck tunic uniforms and Barnett added to this with a summer uniform. He lowered the ratio of police to civilians from a high of 1:1258 down to 1:1000 plus 50 and based the departments recruiting policies around that figure. This lowered further subsequently. This meant an intake of 300 recruits per year for four years then 200 per year thereafter.

He introduced civilian typists throughout the country, getting the police away from their one-fingered typing and out on the street where they belonged.

Barnett initiated a programme to lower the age of retirement from 65 to 60 years, something that became law in the Police Act 1958. Funny how the worm turns, the age was dropped further in 1985 to 55 years or 32 years' service, meaning ex-cadets who started in the police at 17 could theoretically "retire" at 49 years of age.

Subsequently with the introduction of age discrimination legislation, the age limit was abandoned with the police still having some members serving into their 70s.

A Director of Medical Services was appointed and charged with conducting initial medicals for recruits and an ongoing programme of medical checks for serving staff.

A civilian Director of Education Services was responsible for the syllabus and ongoing In Service Training of serving staff. Core education subjects also became part of the Training School syllabus in an effort to lift the literary and numeracy skills of those recruits who needed it.

Training was the hot topic with the new Police Training School being set up at Trentham Military Camp in 1956. There was training during World War 2 for policewomen at the old training school in Colombo Street and later well-known Commandant of the Trentham Police Training School, Ted Hotham, ran a training depot in old navy barracks in Lyttleton prior to the Trentham facility opening. There was no police training at all during the Second World War other than for women police, the consequences keenly felt in the years following.

Recruiting was placed in the hands of competent Sergeants in districts charged with running recruitment programme, interviewing and testing prospective applicants and setting an example of what was expected of a New Zealand Police Officer.

The case of two young Maori men, Murdoch Harris and Donald Ruka, a couple of drifters with criminal tendencies, arrived in Auckland from their Northland homes, committing petty thefts and generally being a bit of a nuisance identified the need for stronger training in the area of interviewing for CIB members.

Both were charged following a series of burglaries and both alleged that they were beaten and intimidated by CIB staff when making statements. Following the high jinks of the previous few years these allegations were taken very seriously by the police and by the Court.

A further Inquiry was started under the chairmanship of Magistrate W H Carson. The most serious allegations were disproved with the complainants admitting fabrication. However the Inquiry revealed a serious and unacceptable deficiency in the police knowledge of law and procedure in the case. Although the members of the CIB involved were exonerated by the Inquiry only a year later two of those named, a Detective Sergeant and an Acting Detective received prison sentences after demanding money with menaces from Chinese opium smokers. Senior police were shocked at the sympathy shown to these two by fellow officers. It was a clear open and shut case with no doubts. This showed that corruption could breed in an atmosphere of complacency and poor training.

Barnett revolutionised the New Zealand Police, putting it on track for further developments in training, human resources, building programmes, transport, specialist squads etc in the coming years. National went out of power in 1957 with Labour taking the reins. Barnett did not get on well with the Labour government. He resigned and went on to other roles as a senior Mandarin in the public service.

Upon Barnett's resignation the Minister appointed Willis Brown as Controller of Police prior to him becoming the first serving police Commissioner since Compton in 1958. Barnett is remembered fondly by retired members who served back in those days. He was solely responsible, together with an understanding Minister, Holland, and an open cheque book, in modernising the police. Out of very bad times good times eventually arrive.

His time in the police also gave younger high-ranking and talented Commissioned Officers time to develop to the point where the police could be handed back to sworn staff in safety and with the confidence of the Government.

Maori in Policing

Prior to European settlement Maori, of course, had their own code of social control and enforcement of law and order. This was usually administered by the chiefs and normally could be quite fatal for offenders.

Once Europeans arrived there were strong efforts by the colonial government to employ Maori police in an attempt to police their own people, act as guides and to encourage assimilation of Maori into the European way of doing things. Maori, however, were not welcomed by many European in the Armed Police Forces of the provinces due basically to racism and reluctance for Europeans to have Maori Constables physically touch and contain them as prisoners.

Turnover of Maori staff was high, probably similar to European staff but for different reasons. However Maori police persisted, especially in the Flying Columns of the Armed Constabulary, as Kupapa chasing the likes of Te Kooti, often under European officers but with the notable exception of Major Kemp or Kepa of Whanganui who commanded his own column of Kupapa.

Maori began to be used as District Constables and, by 1880, there seemed to be no permanently appointed Maori police in the colony, such police being part time District Constables or maybe Runanga Police employed and supervised by tribal authority.

William Carran, dubbed a "Half Caste" when he joined the Police in 1920 seemed to be the first permanently appointed Maori Constable since 1880. Others of part Maori descent may have joined but as European, keeping their Maori connections quiet.

William was a highly successful policeman. He was born on the family property at Bell block, Taranaki on 3 August 1898, one of at least 12 children. He was of the Puketapu hapu of Te Ati Awa, his mother was Ngarongo Kahau and his father Raniera Karena.

He joined the police in Wellington as a Constable, one of few Maori then recorded as serving, the others being five Native and eight District Constables, none of whom were regarded as permanently appointed.

He was posted in quick succession to Otaki (1923), Ngaruawahia (1929) and Kawhia (1932, all districts with high Maori populations. In 1924 he had married Ann McRobie, a nurse. He understood Maori but chose to pursue a European way of life.

William was promoted to Sergeant in 1937 and the family returned to Wellington where he enjoyed a strong reputation as a strict enforcer of the liquor laws: the front of his house in Ohiro Road having to be rebuilt following an explosion that was linked to this aspect of his duties.

In 1943 he was promoted to Senior Sergeant, taking over Taranaki Street police station in 1945 where he was renowned for his firm discipline.

In 1948 he was promoted to Sub-inspector and transferred to Auckland, then to Rotorua in 1946. William was the first Maori to achieve commissioned rank in the modern New Zealand Police. He continued his trek around New Zealand with Ann and the children when he was promoted to Inspector at Timaru in 1950.

He then took command of the Nelson district in 1952 and gave evidence to the 1954 Royal Commission of Inquiry which led to radical changes in the way the police were to operate.

In July 1955 he was promoted to Superintendent and took over the Wellington police district. He was the first New Zealand commissioned officer to be appointed Chief Superintendent in 1958, taking charge of Auckland district followed by Assistant Commissioner later that year in Wellington. Poor Ann must have despaired at all the shifting. William served as deputy to Commissioner Willis Brown until retirement on 23 August 1960. Sadly, a few weeks later, on 1 October 1960, he was killed in a level crossing collision with a locomotive in Whanganui on the way from his son's house in the city to a spot of fishing.

William was a successful police officer at all levels and was very proud of his Maori heritage, leading the way for other Maori to follow his example.

William's success did indeed lead to an increase in the number of young Maori men and women to be permanently appointed as Constables. However whilst Maori have long been officially eligible to join the police on the same terms as Pakeha prejudice against them ensured that they were, apart from William Carran, virtually excluded for the first half of the 20th century. There also seemed to be a reluctance on behalf of young Maori to really consider policing as a career. With the exception of Native and District constables working as auxiliary and part-time members of the police, by 1945 just one Native Constable remained Rawiri (Dave) Hira at Te Kaha and one Maori District Constable, Louis (Heke) Bidois at Te Whaiti. They were that year made Temporary Constables and Hira transferred to Ruatoria and Bidois to Rotorua.

No active attempts were made until the mid-50s to recruit Maori into the police. This changed at the insistence of the Controller-General, Samuel Barnett. He wanted 25 of the first 100 places of the first recruit wing at the new Trentham Police Training School to be reserved for Maori. Fourteen Maori men and two Maori women trained in 1955-56 with two more, too young to become Constables, training in a separate one-off scheme.

After this there is little evidence of further targeting of Maori for Police employment until 1965. By then there were 69 Maori in the police including a number of NCOs. All were very highly regarded by the then Commissioner C L Spencer.

It is clear that despite the evidence, many Maori did join the Police quietly and without fanfare from 1956 to 1965. I recall many great Maori police who were highly respected and looked up to by young staff, Daphne Pomare, Hapeta (Hoppy) Hodges, Tata Parata, Rana Waitai, Stan Hooper, Devon Paaka, Whiro Ratahi and Aporo Joyce being a few I worked with as a youngster in Lower Hutt and Wellington the early 1970s. The one thing they had in common was their exceptional ability in their roles.

An example of probably inadvertent but blatant racism is outlined in the following quote from Spencer's successor in 1965, G.C. Urquhart when he said the following:-
"...that New Zealanders and Maoris is what they should stick to. White races, Americans, South Africans – if they are naturalised and appear when they get here to be acceptable to the New Zealand Police... After further discussion, Mr Urquhart felt that, apart from special circumstance, (the Police should) stick to New Zealanders and Maoris" –

It was felt at the time by the section heads involved in the discussion that *"Hindus, Chinese and others, even if they were British subjects, would be unlikely to fit in".*

One year later recruiting officers were told bluntly that Pacific Islanders *"were not to be considered".*

Of course, from the late 1960s, under the guidance of a far-sighted and enlightened officer, Inspector Brian Davies, the national co-ordinator of recruiting, this all changed with the active recruiting of Maori between 1967 and 1974.

As at 2016 12.3% of New Zealand's police identified as Maori and it was stated that the goal to be reached by 2020 was 15.2%, a huge improvement on the state exactly 100 years before in 1920 when William Carran was the only known permanently appointed Maori police officer in New Zealand.

New Zealand's police is now made up of many cultures thankfully, increasingly reflecting the make-up of today's New Zealand population.

Background to the New Zealand Police Association
1840 to 1913

This is the story of the background to the police union known as the New Zealand Police Association, a body set up to look after the rights and working conditions of all police from Constable to Senior Sergeant. It is the potted story of working conditions for New Zealand police starting in about 1840 and finishing with the formation of the Association in 1936 after nearly 100 years of rigid discipline, martinet officers, hide-bound attitudes and heartless management of an already grossly underpaid and under-privileged workforce charged with keeping the peace in New Zealand.

You may be surprised to know that police have no right to strike and never have had. All police are sworn to the ancient public office of Constable, the legal designation they keep until their discharge no matter what rank is achieved. Even the Commissioner of Police in New Zealand is a Constable under the relevant legislation. This is why, in the years gone by, when any vacancy for Commissioner was advertised in the New Zealand police Gazette the odd wag from the ranks would apply, usually some Constable or Sergeant taking the Michael out of the administration of the police.

Life was grim for police prior to the late 1950s. After that a police officer's working conditions were average only and pay scales were kept low to reflect the fact that being a cop was a working class occupation. Conditions improved drastically from the early 1970s onwards thankfully but when I joined in 1970 police were still required to apply for permission to marry and, if single, had to live in barracks in the main centres. Police were not allowed to have interests in race horses or licensed premises and were still required to attend pay parade as needed, exceptions being granted grudgingly for members on annual leave.

The roster we worked was physically challenging with frequent shift changes so the body never really learned to rest. We would start a late shift at 1.00 p.m. and, theoretically work until 9.00 p.m. I say theoretically as invariably we would work overtime, unpaid of course. We then had to go home, wherever that may be, rest, and be back at parade at 5.00 a.m. the following morning. If one was lucky one would get between four and five hours sleep between shifts. Thankfully this roster was eventually recognised and acknowledged as dangerous to health and dumped for a more civilised shift roster.

From 1840 to about 1900 the working conditions for cops were terrible to say the least. In 1898 a Royal Commission of Inquiry into the New Zealand Police Force was formed by the Premier, Richard Seddon partly due to pressure from the anti-licensing lobby over police neglecting to enforce the licensing laws. Like all Royal Commissions at that time, this commission was set up to investigate, make some recommendations, but really maintain the status quo. To the surprise of many it made huge, far-sighted recommendations to the government which were still being implemented well into the 1950s.

The Commission reported thus, recommending a police pension be paid:-
"The Police Force differs from other branches of the public service. Policemen for many years have had to do dreary night duty, and it appears from evidence that, although they are men of superior physical development there is a tendency to break down at an age at which other government employees are still vigourous. Their occupation exposes them to great risks of injury and disablement. The duty of a Policeman appears to unfit him for any other kind of work, and he must retire at a comparatively early age if the Force is to be an efficient one. For these reasons we strongly recommend the establishment of a Police pension scheme."

Up until 1985 Police retired at 60 years of age. At the time of the commission police usually carried on until they died or were forced out due to ill-health as there was no pension scheme to support them in retirement. Other public servants such as railway staff, had a pension scheme but it was not considered needed or indeed desirable for police to have a pension for some class-ridden reason. They had no union representation so could do little about it. Anybody who spoke up was either told "if you don't like the job, leave" or if particularly persistent and troublesome, just dismissed out of hand, job lost.

Sadly it was my experience in the 1970s and 1980s that many police passed away shortly after retiring at 60, worn out by the years of shift work as young men with few days off. In the early 1980s it was recognised that 60 was too old for sworn police to be employed and the retirement age was lowered further to 55 years or 32 years' service. This saw a large exodus of older sworn staff from the police and, with the Police Early Retirement Fund (PERF) provisions also coming into force, many unfit police also managed to leave with enough savings to support themselves or begin again in another occupation.

These provisions dated from 1985 have their genesis in the far-sighted 1898 Royal Commission and the efforts of the New Zealand Police Association, formed eventually in 1936.

Sadly, since then, with the introduction of age-discrimination legislation the police cannot force a person to retire if that person is still performing his or her duties satisfactorily. This has resulted in police still working on the street in their early seventies, I am not sure if that is a good idea. To be fair to the Police it is the member's choice to work on, they can retire if they wish.

Life was very different for the Sergeant and four Constables who accompanied Governor Hobson from Sydney to Russell in 1840 to act as the colony's first police. In practice they were really Hobson's bodyguard.

The Chief Police Magistrate at the time, Willoughby Shortland, was authorised to hire Constables at .33 cents per day, Sub-Constables at .28 cents per day, lower than the daily rate for the lowest labourer. Those drawn to policing were tradesmen either out of work or unable to get any, usually because they drank too much. A month after Hobson arrived a police boat crew deserted over low pay at Russell. This is the first strike recorded in New Zealand history. The strikers were imprisoned for a month so the first police in New Zealand were also amongst the first gaolbirds. Things did not improve going forward with most Constables lasting only a short time, many being dismissed due to drink or leaving when obtaining better paid work, which was probably not hard if you were not a drunk.

So this was the glorious start of the profession of law enforcement in New Zealand.

It was indeed common for police not to be paid at all for months on end due to the colony's dire financial circumstance. Pay-cuts were even introduced. These men had no days off, paid for their own uniforms and could just be dismissed out of hand for the slightest infraction or at the whim of the local Police Magistrate or other person in authority. In later years, under the Provincial Police system, the Armed Constabulary and the New Zealand Police Force men could be transferred out of hand, married or single, at the slightest whim of officers.

Drink was a continual cause for police dismissals. With no days off the policeman who drank was normally deemed drinking on duty, end of career.

New Zealand was awash with booze back then, probably

nothing much has changed. It was a man's society, a rough, frontier lifestyle, dangerous to say the least. Death was always close to hand either via accident or war. The men who became police were, in the most part, as rough and ready as the men they were required to police. Most were illiterate or semi-literate single men, foot-loose and care-free.

By the time of the 1898 Commission the police in New Zealand had gone through various changes in form and force, as can be read elsewhere. In 1886 the national New Zealand Police Force was founded. It was manned by a mixture of ex-military and ex British police, particularly ex Royal Irish Constabulary members. It was still an under-manned, under-resourced and ill-trained body of men who, if not trained by overseas forces, learned their craft "on the beat" from other, older staff.

Neither the military men nor the RIC men were particularly suitable for the style of non-coercive policing needed by the late 19th century after the New Zealand Wars had petered out, neither won nor lost by either side.

The 1898 Royal commission addressed the resentments of the previous 60 years. The poor pay, harsh discipline and rapid transfers were all summed up in in the example of the married policeman who was declared "insolent" when he objected to nine transfers in 14 years.

Police had had to watch the general public, men only, become enfranchised but had been denied the vote on the grounds that they numbered soldiers among their ranks and soldiers could not be permitted to vote. They were so understaffed by 1896 that they had sunk to the lowest ever ratio of police to population, one to 1530, and copped blame for not controlling the colony's terrible drinking habits. The commission found that police numbers had not kept pace with the growth of the colony. Discipline was poor because there were not enough Sergeants to enforce it. The old Armed Constabulary ethos did not did not fit in with "modern" policing methods.

Seddon's government had imported retired New Scotland Yard Chief Inspector John Tunbridge to oversee new policing methods and then to work with the commission to ensure that the London bobby image would be put in place.

It was recommended that police be recruited from the public, not the military, trained before deployed, uniforms be paid for by the government, a pension scheme put in place and a compulsory retiring age of 60 years introduced (65 for Inspectors) to weed out those no longer up to the job and to stimulate promotion prospects for younger staff.

Recommendations are one thing, implementation is another. Many of these changes took decades to make, Ann Hercus, police minister in the 1980s Labour government, was still trying to make changes nearly 90 years after the commission.

Any improvement was doled out as and when the powers that be felt moved to. There was no machinery for men to air grievances and membership of any union or the formation of any "combination" would and did result in disciplinary action. Tunbridge did his best but was hampered by the use of influence from prominent citizens amongst politicians. His career came to an end when he investigated the acquittal of a Sergeant in Nelson on a charge of drunkenness. Having let the Sergeant off with a warning, and reprimanded and fined two Constables involved, Tunbridge soon found he was not the sole authority in discipline matters, as would be expected as Commissioner. Seddon's cabinet responded to local pressure by derating the Sergeant and requiring the two Constables to resign. Tunbridge was left with little choice but to resign "due to ill-health".

Further scandal beset his successor Walter Dinnie, another British import, over the employment of a constable with a prior conviction, "extreme leniency" with policemen guilty of heavy drinking and the old charges of political influence in the force and inconsistent and unfair promotions. Christchurch prohibitionist and MP, Thomas Taylor, drove these matters, believing that the police were a drunken and totally corrupt lot. Dinnie resigned as well in 1909 and Under-Secretary for Justice, Frank Waldegrave took over the police until 1 April 1912 when John Cullen was appointed Commissioner by the Reform government of William Massey.

As can be seen elsewhere in this book, Cullen, despite being the first Commissioner to rise from the ranks in New Zealand, was no pushover for men who wanted to improve working conditions.

Cullen was also forward-thinking in some ways. He pushed through the Police Force Act of 1913. This included the introduction of qualifying examinations for promotion, tighter disciplinary provisions, a new pay scale; new appeal and inquiry provisions. However the new regulations also required policemen to drill in their time off, a return to military-style policing.

The police still fell mainly out of the working class and were very uneasy about breaking strikes and protecting scabs, some of whom, they knew to be crooks. They were forced to endure abuse from trade unionists who perceived them as the heavy arm of the law but did not enjoy many of the working conditions other workers took for granted by then.

Background to the New Zealand Police Association
1913 to 1936

The Auckland Star announced on 12 April 1913 "Constables Want a Union to Better Their Life". This rocked the police administration to its core. Men met at Trades Hall in Auckland to air their grievances. A summary of such was outlined to the Star. Those on the beat objected to the "constant encroachment made by the Department on the private life and time of the men". A Constable normally did eight hours a day but in reality a great deal more. There was no recognition for this in either pay or time off. A man might be on duty from 0500 hours to 0900 hours and then 1300 hour to 1700 hours. If he made an arrest in the first shift he had to attend Police Court to give evidence which left him little or no time to have a break or eat properly. Having to drill on his one day off in four or five weeks, usually a Sunday, proved the last straw.

The minister of Justice and Police, Alexander Herdman, had only one response to organised complaints: "This sort of thing will not be tolerated". He and Commissioner Cullen fronted the 70 Constables involved in Auckland to hear their grievances. The two were told menial labourers could earn twice as much then as police, up to $1.60 per day. Furthermore police had to pay a mess bill of 3 guineas a month ($6.30), $5.00 per annum for uniform and laundry and increasing amounts for boot upkeep. From these figures it appears a Constable earned in the vicinity of $5.60 per 7 day week, not a lot, even then, to exist on. Married men also had to pay rent.

Nothing was done of course other than the statement being made by Cullen that it was all a matter of money. New Zealand-wide discontent was forcing the administration of the police to address issues. What did they do? Well a Reform government had little time for unions or the cares of the working man so they did what was expected of their class, denied there were any substance to the grievances and transferred the first Police Association secretary Charles Gordon Smyth from Auckland to Greymouth as he was now regarded by his Sergeant and officers with distrust.

Within the month of arriving at his new posting Smyth was dismissed for a minor breach of regulations, namely leaving his post and making a false entry in the time book. Usually such an offence was dealt with by the local Inspector by way of a $1.00 fine.

A similar charge in Auckland just before Smyth's dismissal results in a .50c fine. These figures sound petty nowadays but this was a lot of money for a working man in 1913.

There were continual grievances in the following years, denied by Cullen and following Commissioners. This first attempt at the formation of a Police Association in 1913 was smashed by the Reform government and Commissioner Cullen. One of the Constables involved in this sorry episode was later to become Commissioner himself, John Bruce Young. He was also very instrumental in helping to get the fledgling New Zealand Police Association actually off its feet in 1936 whilst a Chief Detective with the approval of Labour police Minister Peter Fraser.

Labour was the saviour of the working man, police included, from 1916 onwards and then in its first government from 1935 to 1949. Several Labour politicians, later Ministers, had experienced the wrath of the state during World War One, being jailed for sedition, including Peter Fraser and Mickey Savage. One would consider that they had no time for police but this was far from the truth, they were bigger men than that, knowing that most police wanted better working conditions and certainly deserved them compared to other occupational groups.

Whilst the wished for Association did not get off the ground this did not stop grievances continuing. With the beginning of World War One in 1914 police patriotically put their grievances to one side for the better good. Duties changed dramatically with the coming of war, almost half New Zealand's eligible young men were in uniform and off overseas.

Emergency Regulations required police to work longer hours in worse conditions, maintaining surveillance on those left behind. The minister took this outbreak of patriotism and temporary lack of grievances as a sign that the police were fine and morale was high, reporting such to Parliament. Herdman was the Minister of deferral, never making a decision unless he had to, saying that he must "look into it". The matter of the introduction of women police highlighted this. He offered to survey other countries including Australia and the USA, to see what they had achieved but then did nothing.

In 1916 Cullen retired as Commissioner not long after the Kenana Affair and John O'Donovan was appointed. O'Donovan is remembered in police circles most famously for saying that every Constable potentially carried the Commissioner's baton, meaning that even the lowest newest Constable walking the beat could, under the system of policing then in vogue, rise to Commissioner, something that, thankfully has not changed in over 100 years.

At this period police members under the rank of Sub Inspector could join the Public Service association as a sop to the concept of a police only union. By 1922 the relationship with the PSA was not working that well for police. In July of that year 50 police from Wellington resigned their PSA memberships. This was a result of police pay being cut when police were already very poorly paid. Other police around the country stayed on the grounds of collective bargaining ability and the PSA announced that, if it could be shown that the police wanted their own organisation, it would help.

Two-thirds of the police then indicated they wanted to leave the PSA. The PSA then decided that it did not want to represent the police in their attempts to achieve their own union – "no good purpose could be gained by proceeding with Police matters" was the statement made at that year's PSA conference. All police members of the PSA drifted out of the organisation and were the totally without an industrial mouthpiece.

Again there was trouble for members who dared complain, District Commanders would not pass on grievances to the Commissioner and complaining police were targets for attention.

A classic example of having too much too say was the case of Constable William Dunlop Thom. Thom resigned at the start of World War One to go to war. He re-joined in 1919 and like most police then, joined the PSA. He became secretary of the Wellington Police Branch and for three successive years he was the delegate for Wellington City at the annual PSA conference. The other police delegate at the time was John Bruce Young, now representing West Coast Police after his transfer to Greymouth in 1920.

Upon the police leaving the PSA in 1922 Thom thought he had the good wishes of the Wellington members to set about forming a police association. He organised letters to every police station in the country and three-quarters of those surveyed were in favour of forming a police association. Thom was not supported in Auckland, at that time it was reported in the press that Auckland police wanted to stay in the PSA.

Thom appeared before then Commissioner Wright with PSA support to discuss forming a police association. Wright produced the newspaper cutting showing that the Auckland staff was not unanimous in their wish for an association. The interview lasted two minutes with Thom getting short shrift from Wright. The repercussions of that stand would dog Thom for the rest of his police career. The following morning he was told he was being transferred from Wellington. He had a choice, picking Feilding and was sent immediately, leaving his wife recovering from surgery in Wellington Hospital. This was a normal example of how heartless the administration of the police could be. Some may say not much has changed at times.

Old Thom transferred around a bit and eventually became a Sergeant in Dunedin. Being a person of strong mind he led a delegation of Sergeants before the District Commander concerning a shift work hardship matter. He was demoted forthwith to Constable and was alleged to have written an anonymous note and transferred to the sole station at Ross on the West Coast. This allegation was later disproved by a handwriting expert but nothing changed. He was too militant to have around any other serving police and too clever to get dismissed.

The favourite phrase used by Senior Sergeants around 1922 to moaning staff was "if you don't like it, get out". A third of those who joined in 1922 did just that. I can remember that sentiment expressed in the 1970s by certain Sergeants and Senior Sergeants so not much changed in the following 50 years.

The Truth newspaper, always an organ that liked to attack the establishment, including the police, began acting as the lowly cop's unofficial mouthpiece in the 1920s, allowing police to write using nom de plumes. Complaints included uncompensated overtime, police boxers being debarred from public contests, free afternoons forfeit for parades, 12 hour days still being worked despite the introduction of 8 hour shifts, beat men still only getting one Sunday a month off work. Remember, at this time police only got one day per month off and that was not guaranteed.

On 8th September 1923 Truth asked *"Can men who are required to work broken time for 15 hours per day be expected to be alert? And what about the effect on their families who do not see them until 10.00 p.m. at night? This sweated police force is a distinct menace to society and an encouragement to crime"*

Police had support in Parliament, especially amongst the Labour members. John A Lee, no particular lover of the police, said "there should be a channel through which police officers can make representation to the Government of the day for necessary increases in pay and for the rectification of grievances".

D G Sullivan talked of pay scales which saw a Constable with three years' service on $1.50 per day whereas the lowest labouring wage was $1.57 per day.
I
t was clear that the Labour Party, in opposition, were in the frontline police's corner about pay and working conditions.

1935 was to see Labour's first government. It would stay in power until 1949 and introduce a world-beating social welfare, health and housing scheme for working and poor people throughout New Zealand. Peter Fraser was made Minister of Police by Prime Minister Michael savage, a post Fraser would hold and enjoy for some years.

Back to old Thom. He was still stationed in Dunedin when Labour came to power but got transferred in ignominy to Ross before Labour could help him. As stated above he eventually managed to find another handwriting expert who opined that he did not write the note he was alleged to have about a subject he was not interested in and about an incident he was not involved in. He remained in the wilderness for the rest of his career, retiring as a Constable at Islington, near Christchurch in 1954. He had been a Sergeant and was qualified by exam for promotion to Senior Sergeant but was a man of ideas and ideals, a strong supporter of the working-man's rights and, obviously, a pain in the backside of the administration, losing his stripes and sent to Coventry on trumped up charges. He commented that he felt he could have achieved high rank if he had been allowed to.

After the Association in 1936 was set up he was advised to have his case re-opened and was offered financial assistance. His wife was not well and she was very distressed about going through another tribunal matter. This, coupled with the fact that Thom was now broke, decided him to drop the matter.

On Thursday, 8 August 1936 a deputation of police of Senior Sergeant rank and below met with Police Minister Peter Fraser with a proposal to form an Association. Fraser said there was no need for a proposal, since it had already been approved. Three days later seven MPs asked Fraser whether the government was prepared to consider favourably the formation of a police association. Fraser said yes, adding that the government welcomed it and would do everything possible to help.

Affected police were dumbstruck; they had never heard such words of encouragement from a government before.

After many meetings and gaining approval from most members of police below the rank of Sub-Inspector a meeting was held by district delegates in Wellington on 5 August 1936. The result of the meeting was a letter written to the minister by Chief Detective John "Bruce" Young that the association they sought was going ahead without any antagonism to the department and would have no political purpose or connection with any political or industrial organisation. Its objectives were to promote the general welfare of the service and the conditions of its members, particularly in regard to housing, wages, hours of duty and other working conditions. It was already accepted that this group was not for the commissioned ranks, spelling the end of Young's own active involvement upon his eventual promotion to sub-Inspector. Ranks of Sub-Inspector and above later formed their own Officer's Guild which still exists in some form today.

Matters proceeded from there with the New Zealand Police Association coming formally into being on 28th October 1936. The rest is history.

The first Secretary-General of the Association was Ian Drummond Campbell, a lawyer. He was succeeded in 1940 by Jack Meltzer, another lawyer but of a different stamp. Whereas Campbell was a donnish type, Meltzer was an aggressive operator, befitting his interest and participation in boxing. He managed to get well under the skin of Commissioner Denis Cummings during the war years to the extent that Cummings would have nothing to do with him, preferring to talk to the President, Bruce Young, by then a Chief Detective and still subject to direction from "superior" officers..

The full history and development of the New Zealand Police Association is set out in David McGill's excellent book, No Right To Strike. – 1992 – Silver Owl Press.

Most police, upon joining also joined the "Association" after its formation. There were exceptions but these were very few. The Police association is a large organisation nowadays, far from the very small operation set up in 1936. The Association is still headed by a serving police officer who, nowadays, is seconded to the Association from the Police, retaining his or her rank but receiving an increased salary package to reflect the responsibility of having to hold the Commissioner of Police to account and to deal with him or her as an equal. Upon completing the presidential term the incumbent can then return to the Police in his or her old rank if they wish.

The modern day Police Association web-site outlines its purpose as follows:-

"We are an association working to ensure the best employment, health and welfare outcomes for our members and their families – on duty and off duty.

"Our vision is to be the trusted guardian of the wellbeing of the police family. We do this by representing and supporting our members through a combination of advocacy and industrial expertise, and by providing cost effective and well-managed welfare products.

"We have 11,500 members comprising 99% of constabulary police officers across all ranks and 75% of Police employees. That collective strength gives us credibility to advocate for our members in the public domain, with politicians and with Police.

"The fight for fair pay, resources and safe working conditions for NZ police officers began in 1913, and in 1936 the NZ Police Association was legally formed. Now, more than eighty years later, the ever-changing nature of police work presents a myriad of demanding and often dangerous challenges for our members.

"Our members' interests are represented at national level by elected board members, and at the regional level by elected committees."

A History of Women in Policing in New Zealand

The history of women working in the New Zealand police is a history beset by prejudice, sexism, extremely conservative senior police and politicians and a reluctance for many male police to recognise women as their equals as police officers. There has always been a female involvement in policing going back to the earliest days of policing. Wives of police were used to care for and search female prisoners, feed prisoners, take messages if their husband was away on duty and generally support the police on an unpaid basis.

This situation probably still exists to some extent in sole and two-man stations throughout the country, the wife of a country cop is expected to step up and help. Nowadays there may be some way of paying for this, usually by paying the wife as the station cleaner, a token payment for the actual work done.

Whilst New Zealand was probably the last developed English-speaking country to introduce sworn but temporary women Constables in 1941, plain clothed until 1952, New Zealand may have been one of the first, if not the first country to employ a female detective.

There is considerable debate world-wide about who employed the first women police with Chicago claiming first place with Marie Owens in 1893. However in 1891 Richard Bell was murdered in Lora Gorge in Southland. He was shot in the face but lived long enough to name a neighbour John McRae as the offender. The two men were often in dispute over stock issues and illegal alcohol manufacture, a big activity in those days in Southland with clandestine whisky distilleries doing a roaring trade.

The murder investigation was badly handled by police from the start with the local Constable, Hans Rasmussen, reporting the murder to District Headquarters in Dunedin rather than his supervisor in Invercargill, resulting in unnecessary delays and ongoing dispute between detectives and uniform police involved subsequently in the enquiry. McRae was arrested but there was nothing definite other than Bell's statement to connect him to the crime, McRae denying any knowledge. The Lora Gorge area community was very close-knit and suspicious of police generally and outsiders anyway. The community was made up of poor farmers of Scottish Highland origin with a natural dislike of authority.

The police were getting nowhere when Ursula Smith, a 20 year old actress, offered her services to the police as an undercover detective. She would go to the area disguised as a 15 year old from town sent to live with a trusted family in the area for health reasons. She would try to become friendly with one of McRae's young sons and try to glean information about the murder through her relationship with the boy. In the interim a male detective was placed in the area as a swagman but was quickly identified as police. After an initial reluctance to employ Smith the Commissioner at the time, Hume, agreed. Ursula Smith wrote a formal letter setting out her conditions and expected salary. She was a very forthright and brave young woman for her time. She was engaged at one pound per week with a further pound per week for living expenses. After further bargaining and being attested, Detective Smith travelled to Lora Gorge to stay with the Taylor family as Bessy Nichol, the niece of Mr Taylor.

McRae was released without charge at a depositions hearing. Detective Smith as Bessy formed a close relationship with Donald McRae, the 15 year old son of the suspect McRae. They met frequently at the McRae home or went walking in the countryside.

Donald named another local, James Trender, as the murderer of Bell. Trender was rumoured to be having affairs with Bell's wife and with her daughter at the same time. Despite Smith's persistent questioning Donald revealed nothing further that could help implicate Trender.

Detective Smith had to leave Lora Gorge soon after as another boarder was expected at the Taylor home. Records show that if Smith had managed to stay longer it was the opinion of the local district commander, Inspector Pardy, that the investigation into Trender would have been ultimately successful. There was an ongoing and strong belief in the community that the police had let Trender get away with murder.

Smith returned to "domestic duties" at her home in Campbelltown (Bluff) and carried on with acting parts in local dramas and plays. She offered herself again to act as a decoy to catch a man assaulting women in Dunedin but this offer was declined *"...as it was generally thought that detective work was too dangerous for a woman".*

Ursula Smith certainly qualifies as New Zealand's first woman detective and may well have been the first person in the world to be employed by a police service in this capacity, a year before Marie Owens in Chicago, USA.

This early foray into policing by women in New Zealand went no further for at least another 20 years, until the time of the First World War. Despite New Zealand women being the first women in the world to receive the vote in 1893 women were kept shut out of all public offices and most professions until well into the 20th century due to the chauvinistic behaviours and attitudes of those in power back then.

In the meantime police matrons were becoming established

in the larger centres in New Zealand to assist with dealing with female prisoners and children. Matrons remained at large police stations throughout the 20th century. I remember the matron still residing in her flat in Wellington Central police station, above the cell block in the mid-1970s. By that time women police were becoming more common and most shifts had at least one woman Constable who could either assist the matron of act in her place as needed throughout the day and night.

Matrons were usually older women of high respect in the community, sometimes widowed or single, sometimes married. It was common to also be a member of a serving officer's family. They worked within the confines of the police station.

When looking at women in policing there are three basic areas of employment, matrons within stations, non-sworn female staff working as typists, clerks, administrative assistants and in watchhouses as telephone operators and, lastly sworn female Constables permanently appointed with all the powers and almost all of the duties of their male colleagues.

It seems the first two categories, matrons and non-sworn female staff were really not an issue to either the government or the administration of the police but the idea that a woman could be trained and qualify as a Constable, let alone climb the ranks as men could was a "bridge too far" for the conservatively-minded men in charge in the first half of the 20th century.

There seemed to be a feeling that women were not robust enough for police work. I can personally attest to working with many very brave and tough women in the police who never shied from danger. I cannot say that about quite a few male colleagues who were wary about any form of physical confrontation or of entering many dangerous situations.

There was huge pressure on the government during the First World War to employ women police due to the loss to military duties of many male police. Massey's Reform Government, conservative by its very nature, would not agree. The Police Minister Alexander Herdman reported on employment of women police to the Solicitor General on 16 October 1916 as follows:-

"I am of the opinion that there is no power under the present law to appoint women as members of the Police Force. The general principle is that no woman is qualified to hold a public office"

He goes on later to say:-

"the office of constable is , in in my opinion, a public function within the meaning of this rule by reason of the statutory powers possessed by constables. The general principle of disqualification applies unless the legislature has in the Police Force Act 1913 indicated a contrary intention either expressly or impliedly. No such exception can be read into the Act. The nature and purposes of a Police Force indicates sufficiently that it was intended by the Legislature to be a force consisting of men...."

Despite protestations from 21 women's organisations led by Lady Stout, the wife of Sir Robert Stout and a woman of much influence and ability, to Herdman he dug his toes in, dithered, ignored overseas research, especially about the success of women in policing in England. Also significant positive results from experiments in the USA and Canada were placed to one side as well.

It was clear that Massey and Herdman had no intention of allowing women to become constables in the then New Zealand Police Force while they had any say in the matter As a sop or a compromise four Assistant Matrons were appointed in May 1917, women with formal training, especially in nursing. They were allowed to work outside of police stations in situations where young children or young women frequented or were in danger such as parks, railway stations etc. They were not uniformed. They also attended juvenile court when female children were charged with offences.

By 1919 their work in the community had become established. A stop-gap put in place to stop pressure from women's groups?

The Assistant Matrons seemed to be very busy and were carrying the load of constables but without the powers conferred on their male colleagues. Matron diaries from the time show very full days undertaking reactive duties with little time to undertake preventive patrolling, the original main reason for their appointment. Prison escorts, court work, assisting with female offenders in the community, escorting female patients to mental asylums and visiting schools made for very busy Assistant Matrons.

Unsurprisingly the Assistant Matrons came to be held in very high regard by their male colleagues despite the tales of gloom and doom propagated by Herdman and many senior police previously.

Women's groups kept the pressure on however. These were the women or the daughters of women who managed to get the vote in 1893, they simply did not take no for an answer. Many women of influence in the community were members of or led these groups so their self-important but powerful husbands would have had continual badgering at home about their causes. New Zealand was to get women police come hell or high water.

In 1933 Elizabeth McCombs became the first woman to be elected to the House of Representatives after successfully contesting the Lyttleton seat of her late husband's. A member of the Women's Christian Temperance Union, she resurrected parliamentary debate about women police and became the staunchest advocate of the idea. At the time in opposition as a Labour MP, she could do little to affect change but that would change in 1935 when Labour swept to power under Michael Joseph Savage. Peter Fraser was, later in Labour's term, appointed Police Minister, a role he would hold for years, and set about making a few significant changes to policing.

By 1938 a large amount of further research was completed by both the police and Fraser's research assistants which favoured the concept of women Constables. At that time there were only 8 Matrons and Assistant Matrons in the country.

Fraser introduced the Statues Amendment Act 1938 to Parliament, section 45 of the Act providing authority to introduce sworn women police into New Zealand. History is quiet on the response from the police administration but, bearing in mind the conservatism of the times, one can imagine. The then Commissioner D J Cummings was initially very conservative about the idea but gradually warmed.

First the Labour government allows the police rank and file to form a union in 1936, now, two years later; they have approved the appointmen t of women Constables, where will it end. The ructions in the offices of various senior police around the nation would have been interesting to witness.

Positions were advertised by newspaper during 1939. Women had to be unmarried or widowed and between 25 and 40 years of age. They were invited to send their applications, including education background and previous work history to their nearest Superintendent of Police. 150 applications were received. With the outbreak of war in 1939 nothing more was done until June 1941 when the first 10 women Constables began training at the training depot in Rintoul Street, Newtown, Wellington. They were sworn in as Temporary Constables as were all other women accepted in subsequent intakes during the war. A total of 37 women were accepted for training between 1941 and 1944. Several left for various reasons, mainly marriage, so that by March 1946 there were only 29 remaining. The women were working hard to be accepted but there was still resistance from senior police, who simply thought that this was a fad that would disappear with time and attrition.

For the sake of history and to acknowledge these pioneers, the first 10 women appointed Constables, albeit Temporary Constables in 1941 were:-
Lilian Brocket, Nancy Aitchison, Vera McLeonchie, Caroline Smith, May Berridge, Margaret Holder, Edna Pearce, Eileen O'Connor, Molly Speakman and May Callaghan.

Constable Evelyn Owen was the first female Maori Constable appointed in New Zealand in 1943.

All the women had superior education backgrounds for their time, many with nursing or office backgrounds and all were single. The designation of Temporary Constable remained until after the war when all members were then made permanently appointed Constables. During the 1940s and until 1952 the women were not uniformed and worked across all areas of police activity as well as for Special Branch, acting as decoys for sex offenders, catching bookies, normal enquiry work and patrolling. In 1950 a progressive Commissioner John "Bruce" Young was appointed. He advised in November 1952 that all policewomen will be uniformed by early 1953. Behind the scenes there was obviously much going on about how the women were being treated and the lack of recognition they received from some quarters. Young wanted this to stop and putting them in uniform would help them being accepted as the valuable police that they were.

By 1956, when the Controller-General of Police, Samuel Barnett, provided his annual report to Parliament he advised that there were 62 sworn women Constables but that 16 or these Constables had had no formal training. He opined
"women police are not yet playing the important role of which they

are capable within the force. The British policewomen have built a tradition for themselves against a deal of prejudice. New Zealand women have not had quite the same opportunity".

Barnett's time in office saw women police broaden their role within the service.

Since 1956 women police have trained and worked with male colleagues, undertaking the same duties, having the same opportunities for promotion and entrenching their role as vital to the police service of New Zealand.

The road was still bumpy with women who wanted to marry being pressured to leave the police. There are reported examples of female Constables being transferred from a station where the husband remained serving in the Police, thereby separating the couple and trying to force the female to resign from the police. Sadly many women did resign to marry due to the attitudes of their managers and on occasions when forced to transfer away from their husbands. There was at least one instance where the woman stuck to her guns and managed to get transferred back to her original posting. Up until 1972 female police formed the Women's Division, being commonly referred to by other staff as WDs. The term stuck around for many years afterwards, not always as a term of endearment or support by many male police.

In terms of salary women police got paid less than their male counterparts to begin with but by the time I joined in 1970 pay was equal.

Women are now employed in all sworn sections of policing, even the last bastions of male pride, Armed Offender Squads and Dog Section. They perform as well as and usually better than their male counterparts in many aspects of policing. They also tend to do better academically overall for some reason. This has, at last, transformed into women reaching the higher positions in the police. As of writing a woman has yet to be appointed Commissioner of Police but that is only a matter of time.

Alexander Herdman, Commissioner John Cullen and William Massey, and many other conservative, hide-bound male chauvinists in the police, the arch-critics and opponents of women in the police during the First World War and prior to 1938, would not be impressed, I am sure.

I have only touched on non-sworn female staff within the police. The police could not operate efficiently without the large body of non-sworn police who undertake the countless support roles and are employed in professional positions within the police rank structure.

Many non-sworn are female and their roles are diverse, ranging from communications, assisting sworn staff in watchhouses, clerical and typing support, payroll duties, higher management roles, the list is endless. Many family members of sworn staff join the unsworn ranks, some prior to training to become sworn. I had two siblings who worked for the police in unsworn positions, one for many years. As I have said elsewhere, policing can be a family thing.

T

he police would probably cease to function nowadays without female sworn and unsworn staff.

Police Lore
Piss Property and Prostitutes

Piss, property and prostitutes, the three Ps. Every young police trainee hears, or used to hear, these within days of beginning his or her training, usually one of the first lectures delivered by Sergeant or Senior Sergeant Instructors at the police college along with a lecture to the males about leaving the female members of the course to their studies.

A review of the police history texts and the police district histories for New Zealand, going back to the 1840s shows that booze, sticky fingers and the little brain ruling the big brain have all been chronic discipline issues for male police members. Many a career, distinguished, promising or not, has foundered on these three rocks of uncertainty in any budding and, sadly, some senior police officer's careers.

The history books are littered with the tales of drunken cops being fired, locked up or transferred, usually with further transgressions resulting in dismissal. No such thing as treating the cop's drinking problem as a health issue, simply a discipline lapse. The old police in the 1850s to the 1880s were a mixed bunch of semi-literate labourers, leavened with the odd educated person.

For most New Zealand males in those days, including many police, alcohol was the staff of life. Police worked seven days per week, were required to be in uniform at all times with little free time to themselves so the opportunity to grab a beer on the beat was very tempting, especially with friendly licensees seeking to curry favour with the police. Of course many licensees were also ex-police so were sympathetic to the plight of their old colleagues.

One of the reasons for the beat point system was to make sure a Constable was seen by their Sergeant on a regular basis, ensuring that they had little time to linger anywhere, chatting with the public or "inspecting licensed premises".

At least New Zealand did not have a prison just for police as Victoria did. Victorian police could go to jail, serve a sentence in their own prison and, upon release, resume duty. This was usually for minor offences of drunkenness and assault. Thievery resulted in dismissal in both colonies.

Police Regulations, even when I joined in 1970, still described in detail the dangers of drinking on duty, consorting with women of low repute, having no pecuniary interest in licensed premises, sleeping on the beat. Breaches of all these and about 60 other archaic regulations could result in instant dismissal from the police. In reality, by the mid to late 20th century, warnings usually sufficed for such breaches if, indeed, they were even reported by supervisors.

The requirement to seek permission to marry still existed well into the 1970s, put in place to stop constables from marrying those women of low repute, women who had an interest in licensed premises or in race horses and women who were known criminals or consorted with known criminals.

All of the above to protect the virtue of our saintly Constables on the beat, stopping them from falling to the temptation of the bottle or the pleasures of the flesh on cold, winter nights on the beat.

Nowadays police who have a predilection for alcohol are treated for this with a view to retaining their services. Alcoholism is regarded as a health issue now in society, making the police adopt a more understanding stance towards staff. Also the culture of the police seems to have changed in the last 30 years. Up until the 1980s the drinking culture within the police was, like society in general, very strong. Whilst there were good points to this in terms of camaraderie there were also major issues with health and discipline problems at times. Police Canteens are now mostly closed throughout the country, removing the opportunity for drinking after duty for police, a sign of a healthier society no doubt. I am not sure about the camaraderie aspect though.

I have always thought the oldest profession got a bad rap in the story of the three Ps. Sex workers, in my experience, are mostly hard-working street-wise women who either kept well out of the way of police or were looked after in a brotherly or fatherly way by many street cops sharing the streets at night with them. Sex workers are some of the most vulnerable workers in our community and in my experience most decent cops tended to look after them or treat them with kindness and understanding, keeping an eye out for them. There have been other cops who have also taken unfair and unpaid advantage of them to their shame.

I am sure some cops over the years may have sought some paid comfort in the arms of these women as well, as many men do. An unwise move for a serving cop. It is funny how things can get around in a small place like New Zealand.

The term "prostitute" in the story of the "three Ps" really was a misnomer, unfair really, for illicit or unwise liaisons with members of the fairer sex. Extra-marital affairs, cuckolding other men or relationships with women of the criminal underclass could all result in dismissal or a transfer to another station forthwith, usually at the other end of the country and sometimes at the cop's expense. Try explaining that to the wife and kids. Victorian standards of morality for working class people lingered well into the late 20th century in the New Zealand police. Certainly, homosexuality was unforgiveable in a serving officer. Any such transgression would result in instant dismissal and possible imprisonment.

Having seen two very good cops, good mates, lose their careers after being "outed" by jealous partners of their male lovers in the 1970s I was, firstly as surprised as many others but then deeply saddened at the harsh way they were dealt with. At that time homosexual acts between men was still a crime punishable by imprisonment. Thankfully neither man faced this ignominy, perhaps the beginning of some understanding by senior police. They are fine men who went on to have very successful lives but who were very good police officers, both with the potential to reach high rank where they would have been able to influence the police culture for the better in my opinion.

Thankfully the police slowly caught up with the mores of normal society at the end of the 20th century allowing for a more diverse constabulary but the issue of unwise relationships will always be a matter for management and, perhaps, disciplinary action. Sadly police have also been caught up in sexual offending over the years including instances of obscene exposure, stalking, rape and group deviancy. This is all a matter of public record and, without going into details, shows that this is an ongoing issue within the police up to the modern day, resulting in the Commission of Inquiry into Police Conduct which began in February 2004 and reported in 2007.

Many matters have gone to trial, proved or acquitted. Whatever the outcome, invariably the accused's career is over.

Sometimes imprisonment has been the result where charges have been proved.

Of the three Ps, stealing property is a huge breach of trust. Transgression in the handling of property will result in dismissal and possible charges with, until recent years, time inside for the offender.

There is nothing regarded lower within the police culture than a thief. Preservation of property is one of the cornerstones of modern day Western policing. Police are expected to be completely above reproach when it comes to honesty.

Handling found property is a regular duty for any street cop. There is a very strong system in place for dealing with found property and ensuring accountability for it. Any irregularity in property records found by a supervisor will result in a serious inquiry, the first port of call being the Property Officer in large stations or the Constable in small one or two man stations. Many are the times when property has been "lost", resulting in a cop being charged with theft after admitting stealing.

Police were also required to collect monies upon warrant issued by the Courts. This was also a regular temptation for the rare cop with sticky fingers. Sadly some cops steal due to gambling addictions. I have sadly seen Police Bar Managers, serving police, sacked and charged for stealing money from either the police club or the pokie machines. Invariably they have a gambling addiction. Whilst steps will be taken to help them with their addiction this will not be done by the police but by the probation service as part of their sentence as they are sacked and sometimes charged with theft. Many times this is the sad end to a very fine career for an otherwise very good person.

So the three Ps, a trap for young players? No, a constant warning throughout any police career. I have seen cops nearing the end of their long service dismissed or disgraced for drinking issues, sexual misbehaviour or theft, the three Ps. As relevant now as it was back in the 1840s when New Zealand's first police walked the streets of frontier towns.

Whilst most of the examples seen in texts apply to Constables and Sergeants the odd Commissioned Officer also fell afoul of the three Ps, they are no respecter of rank or position in the community. Commissioned Officers would find themselves fired, moved on or retired early.

Demotion was an option for NCOs who transgressed, probably still is. Busted down to Constable for a year or two in another station and then considered forgiven enough to resume working as a Sergeant. There are stories of members moving up and down the classes of ranks and the actual ranks in the late 19th century, seemingly willy-nilly, not only for disciplinary reasons but also to suit the administration of certain districts. One does wonder though whether one of the three Ps was behind it all.

Having been out of the police for nearly 30 years I am not sure if this lecture is now delivered to new students at the Police College. Maybe recruiting standards are much higher now and it is assumed that the average student is above this sort of behaviour. I doubt that very much.

Martin Cash
Cop-killer, Brothel-keeper and Dishonest Policeman

In the 1850s provincial police forces in New Zealand struggled to employ decent men as Constable or Privates. Many Maori were employed as police with a view to helping them integrate into European society with mixed results. The good burghers of the major towns objected to "savages" laying their hands on white people and arresting them. Maori police feature throughout the history of policing in New Zealand and are the subject of a separate chapter. The Canterbury Province Armed Police Force was particularly hard up for decent recruits. Illiteracy and drink were the two overwhelming barriers to getting or retaining police in the province. Christchurch was slowly becoming a town in its own right apart from the port of Lyttleton, a main immigration port. The quality of immigrants varied greatly from genteel society people to the dregs of society, blighted by the presence of "Irish and Scotch". Turnover of staff was high with men resigning to return to labouring which actually paid better money with shorter hours. Many were also dismissed due to unsatisfactory performance or intemperance.

In about 1860 Christchurch was graced with the presence of the well-known and infamous Tasmanian bushranger Martin Cash in the guise of a newly-minted Constable of the Armed Police Force. His history and escapades are well documented by David Green in 1990 in the Dictionary of New Zealand Biography thus:-

"Martin Cash, was from County Wexford, Ireland. He worked there as a farm labourer until March 1827, when he was convicted of housebreaking. Sentenced to seven years' transportation, he served his time as a farm worker in the Hunter Valley of New South Wales, Australia, then in 1837 moved to Van Diemen's Land (Tasmania) with a neighbour's wife, Bessie Clifford. In 1840 he was sentenced to seven years' imprisonment for the theft of eggs

valued at a shilling.

"In the next three years he escaped from gaol three times, on the last occasion from the Port Arthur gaol by swimming shark-infested seas with two comrades. The three outlaws survived by raiding homesteads and settlements to obtain food, money and ammunition.

"Cash's good manners and penchant for robbing the rich earned him the sobriquet 'The Robin Hood of Van Diemen's Land'. He was recaptured, in mid-1843, after the news that his beloved Bessie had left him for another provoked him to look for her in Hobart. Sentenced to death for killing a constable while trying to evade arrest, Cash gained a last-minute reprieve and was sent to Norfolk Island for 10 years. Here he was a model prisoner. He was given some responsibility and was allowed to marry a fellow convict, Mary Bennett, on 14 May 1854. Later in 1854 he was granted a ticket of leave, returned to Van Diemen's Land, and became a constable at the Cascades penal settlement.

"He also worked as an overseer at the government gardens in Hobart, before being conditionally pardoned in 1856. Subsequently he moved to New Zealand, leaving his wife and an infant son in Tasmania.

"In 1860 Cash came to public attention in Christchurch as a constable in the Canterbury Province Armed Police Force, which it appears he had joined the previous year. This gave him inside information useful in his main line of work, brothel-keeping. However, his colleagues had become suspicious of him, and united to convince officials that his identity and activities should be investigated.

In March 1860 Cash was sacked and fined for keeping a brothel, amid fears that many others like him might have chosen to come to New Zealand after the decline of the Australian goldfields.

"Details about Cash's activities after this date are scarce. He appears to have visited Tasmania at the end of 1860, but had returned to New Zealand by December 1862.

"According to one account he continued to operate several brothels in Christchurch's red light district, around Salisbury Street, including the notorious 'Red House', and regularly featured in the court news until unwelcome police attention encouraged him to try his luck on the Otago goldfields.

"There he is supposed to have been detected by the Otago police, and 'advised' to leave the province. According to this story he soon returned to Christchurch, withdrew his ill-gotten savings (allegedly about £2,000) from the bank, and returned to Tasmania. Here in May 1863 he bought a small farm at Glenorchy, a few miles from Hobart, where he lived with his wife and son.

"Towards the end of his life he narrated his autobiography to James Lester Burke, who edited and published it in 1870 under the title The adventures of Martin Cash. He died on 27 August 1877 from 'Fatty degeneration of Heart with Inflammation of Stomach and Intestines accelerated by Intemperance'." – Te Ara Encyclopaedia of New Zealand 1990.

When Cash's fellow-Constables "united" to tell provincial officials about the crooked and seriously criminal policeman in their ranks they did so as a "combination" as, of course, back then, Constables were not to have a voice on matters that affected the running of the police. They obviously felt that there was safety in numbers when they informed on Cash.

This example of a "combination" shows how insecure a Constable's position could be if he spoke up about any matter beyond his purview.

Of course, Cash was not the only bad'un to make it into uniform as a Constable in the colony's police but he is an example of the wild and woolly days of frontier New Zealand and the loose controls on recruiting in a small country being inundated with settlers from Britain, Ireland and the other Australasian colonies.

Wahine Disaster

10th April 1968. Just about anybody with a functioning memory alive today who lived in Wellington on that date will remember where they were that day. It is up there with the assassination of President J F Kennedy in 1963, one of those days in time that stay with one all one's life.

I was a 15 year old fifth former. The previous night was stormy but not too bad but in the morning, whilst getting ready for school I noticed trees falling and roofing iron in the street outside our Naenae home. It was a rough day. My father had gone to work at 6.30 a.m. as usual and he rang to tell my mother to keep us all home from school as the cyclone was only going to get worse. He was home himself at about 10.00 a.m.

We had the radio on in the kitchen and could hear 2ZB broadcast the news that the inter-island ferry TEV Wahine was foundering on Barretts reef at the mouth of Wellington Harbour. In those days we did not have morning television but I recall seeing scenes of the tragedy on TV later in the day. It was an eerie day, terrible weather in the morning, schools closed, workers sent home or staying home, trains unable to run, the streets deserted but by late afternoon my father and I were outside cleaning up in sunshine.

The Union Steam Ship Company's 8948-ton roll-on roll-off passenger ferry WAHINE, the largest ship of its kind in the world when completed two years earlier, left Lyttelton at 8.40 p.m. on the evening of 9 April. There were 734 passengers and crew on board. Storm warnings had been issued, but rough seas were nothing new in Cook Strait. As it turned out, the WAHINE was about to sail into one of the worst storms ever recorded in New Zealand. The ship reached Cook Strait as tropical cyclone Giselle swept south and collided with a southerly front. The combination of warm tropical air and cold air dragged up from Antarctica produced exceptionally violent turbulence.

At 5.50 a.m. on the morning of 10 April Captain H. G. Robertson decided to enter Wellington Harbour. The wind was blowing at over 50 knots, but vessels had entered the harbour in stronger winds before Just as the *Wahine* reached the narrow funnel of the harbour entrance, however, the wind speed suddenly increased to over 100 knots. Shortly after 6 a.m. the *Wahine's* radar system failed and a huge wave slammed into the ship, throwing many of those on board off their feet. Now side on to the towering waves, the vessel was pushed towards the notorious Barrett Reef on the western side of the harbour entrance.

For 30 minutes the *Wahine* fought the waves, as Robertson apparently attempted to turn his ship back out to sea in poor visibility. At about 6.35 a.m., unaware of his location, the captain ordered full astern. At 6.40 a.m. the vessel reversed onto Barrett Reef. The starboard propeller was knocked off, and the port engine stopped shortly after. Initially many of the passengers were unaware of what was happening due to the ferocious battering the ship was receiving from the storm.

With the ship's engines no longer working, Captain Robertson ordered that all watertight doors be closed and both anchors dropped. Passengers were now informed that the ferry had run aground on the reef. The signal station at nearby Beacon Hill was notified of the accident as the crew prepared life-saving equipment. Flooding in four compartments and on the vehicle deck raised serious concerns about the stability of the ship.

The *Wahine* dragged its anchors and gradually drifted further up the harbour past Point Dorset. Despite being close to shore, the weather made it impossible for rescuers to reach the ship from land.

The tug *Tapuhi* set off from Queen's Wharf and reached the *Wahine* at about 11.00 a.m. By 11.50 the tug had secured a line to *Wahine*. An attempt was made to tow the ferry to safety, but the line quickly gave way. Other attempts to get a line to *Wahine* failed. Shortly after noon the deputy harbourmaster, Captain Galloway, managed to climb aboard the *Wahine* from the pilot launch, which had also reached the scene. He risked his life jumping from a heavily pitching launch to a ladder hanging over the starboard side of the ship.

By 1.15 p.m. the *Wahine* was listing heavily to starboard. The tide and storm had swung the ship around so that there was a patch of water sheltered from the wind and waves on the lower starboard side. Just before 1.30 p.m. the order was finally given to abandon ship.

Captain Robertson had resisted this call because he felt that the storm conditions meant it was safer for the passengers to remain on board. He was also keen to avoid causing any unnecessary panic. Passengers, who had been unaware of just how serious the situation was, were now confused and frightened. People slid across the sloping deck, trying to make their way to the lifeboats. Some passengers had removed their life jackets during the morning and were using them as pillows when the order came to abandon ship. Others did not know which side was starboard and instead made their way to the high side of the ship, from which it was impossible to launch the lifeboats.

Only the four starboard lifeboats could be launched, and crewmen tried to get as many people as possible onto them. One lifeboat was swamped shortly after leaving the sinking ship and its occupants were tossed into the sea. (Two of the other lifeboats safely reached Seatoun; the third landed at Eastbourne). Other passengers were forced to jump into the cold, churning sea. Some clung on to inflatable liferafts that had been thrown overboard, but a number of these were punctured by the wreckage or flipped over by the heavy seas.

At about 2.30 p.m. the now-abandoned *Wahine* capsized in 11.6 metres of water just east of Steeple Rock Light and crashed heavily to the seabed. By this time the first of the survivors had already reached the western shore at Seatoun.

The *Wahine* was within sight of land and many other vessels, including the smaller New Zealand Railways Wellington-Picton ferry *Aramoana*, which stood by to pick up survivors. Many survivors were blown across the harbour towards Eastbourne Beach, an area with difficult access. Rescue teams found the road to Eastbourne blocked by slips. Eventually 200 survivors struggled through the surf to safety on this coast, but it was here that most of the 51 fatalities occurred. A number of people who reached shore alive did not receive medical attention quickly enough to prevent death from exposure. Others were drowned or killed when thrown against rocks.

Robertson and Galloway were the last to abandon ship after checking that no one remained on the ferry. They spent an hour in the water near the wreck before being rescued.

Although the stricken *Wahine* was close to New Zealand's capital city, the rescue effort was delayed by several hours due to uncertainty over the ship's fate. Those on shore were only just beginning to realise the gravity of the situation. Emergency services were fully stretched dealing with numerous call-outs as the storm tore roofs off houses, toppled trees and caused injuries as people were hit by flying debris.

Because of slips blocking the road, only eight police officers were initially able to get to Eastbourne. Eventually another 100 officers and 150 civilians were involved in the rescue effort there.

This was a difficult task in appalling weather, and many worked through the night to assist survivors. In all, 371 police members out of a total of 629 in the Wellington district, national headquarters and the training school were involved.

Chief Inspector George Twentyman of Police National Headquarters took charge of co-ordinating the rescue at 2.05 p.m. He had been involved in the 1953 Tangiwai disaster operation where he had observed first-hand the confusion and stress created by handling inquiries in the same place as the rescue effort. He therefore immediately set up separate groups in different locations to handle the various aspects of the operation and allow the rescue effort to go forward unimpeded. Separate points in the city were established to deal with inquiries about the passengers and crew while a survivor assembly station was set up at Wellington railway station. A mortuary and property section was also established.

Events at Tangiwai had also been hampered by the fact that no national civil defence organisation existed. By 1968 this was no longer the case, and a quick mobilisation of local authority, military and civilian volunteer assistance was now possible. The Wellington harbour master controlled the sea rescue.

Whilst the police were mounting a huge rescue operation at Eastbourne and Seatoun on the opposite side of the harbour, amongst the passengers on board the Wahine were several police officers returning from a court case in Christchurch. I got to know most of these men as they were all still stationed in the Wellington area a few years later when I began work as a Constable in the Hutt. Likewise on the Eastern shore were many Hutt cops I would soon get to know as well. The rescue efforts made by these police and other, civilian rescuers, was simply heroic and deeply affected many of them for many years later. I recall attending the farewell of a highly-respected Detective Sergeant in the mid 1990s. In his farewell speech he recalled Wahine Day. He had been on board the ship, swam to the eastern shore and tried to save as many people as he could but lost a few in the sea or some he saved killed on the beach by the power of the waves. He broke down in tears, a giant of a man, scared of no-one.

Two police staff who featured in the 50 year anniversary of the disaster as being involved, one on the shore and one on the ship, outlined their experiences that day to Police Ten One magazine for posterity.

When he realised his lifejacket would keep him afloat, Detective Tata Parata thought he had a good chance of making it to shore. Groups of survivors were congregating together as they drifted toward the Pencarrow coast.

"People were hanging on to their young kids," he says. "One group I was in there was about eight or nine of us. A dad had his little boy by the hand. The little boy had a large-size lifejacket on and where you put your head he had right over his body."

Rubber life rafts designed to hold 25 people blew past them, empty – whipped from people's hands by the gale as they were untied from the Wahine. They were the first things to reach the shore.

From the water Tata could see boats trying to get people aboard – but they lacked rescue gear and were being tossed by monstrous swells which had them one moment five or six metres above their targets, then below them in a trough.

"You were flotsam and jetsam in the big ocean," he says. "You had no choice but to go where you were taken."

Tata was in the water for about 40 minutes. As his group neared the shore the churning sea separated them. "I don't know what happened to those unfortunate people," he says.

It was with huge relief that he felt his feet touch sand. Strong hands grabbed him and hauled him on to the beach. Attached to the hands was his friend and workmate, Constable Hapeta Hodges – known to all as Hoppy.

"He said 'What the hell are you doing here?' He grabbed me and put me down on the beach. I turned around and he was back in the sea and had two people in lifejackets, dragging them both to shore. To this day I don't know what happened to them.

"It was a very odd sort of situation – you go over the side, you get landed on the shore and you get picked up by a work buddy.

Constable Hapeta Watene "Hoppy" Hodges was known for his fitness. He was a keen skindiver. He had been dealing with storm damage in Stokes Valley when he was called to Lower Hutt Police Station.

Soon after arriving he saw lifeboats coming in, with passengers jumping out in panic as they neared the shore. His first rescue was of a woman from one of the boats, holding a baby in the surf.

"She was bawling her eyes out. I went in and took the baby off her and went up to where the police cars were, where I gave the infant back to her. I took my tunic off and gave it to her. I was pleased to get it back because my pay was in the pocket.

"Those guys jumping in who couldn't swim wouldn't have a show because there were some big waves coming in."

Later he had to retrieve one terrified young man from a bush up the hillside, where he had scrambled after getting ashore. "We had to make sure that once he got down he didn't jump back into the water again," he says.

Hoppy wrote an account of his actions which was included in Chief Inspector George Twentyman's report on the operation. He describes going from beach to beach, dragging people from the waves.

Some were dead, and some he suspected were too weak to survive. He estimates the last person he helped was around 5km down the coast road.

He was interested to know if two women he had pulled from the surf in very weakened condition had survived. They had not – he found their bodies as he made his way back toward Burdan's Gate.

"I was so fatigued towards the end of the rescue operation that I could hardly walk to the next raft – let alone run – and in this state of fatigue I was not clearly conscious of how many persons I was pulling out," he wrote.

"I was buggered," he says with less formality, remembering events 50 years later. "It was a hell of a day."

Tata was walking up the coast road, soaked and missing one shoe but glad to be alive. He was exhausted but had just one injury.

"When I came ashore I kind of punched myself in the nose and broke it," he says. "But no other cuts and bruises. Exhausted. Probably over-excited, glad to put my feet on the ground. Glad to have landed on a beach."

He met a number of colleagues – including Constable Tom Penrose.

"I said 'What are you doing here?'," says Tom.

"He said 'I was on the bloody boat'. It was very unusual to hear him swear."

Some thought Tata was a rescuer. "One of the young fellows came along and said 'Parata, what are you doing with that life-jacket on? Put it back'," says Tata. "They had no idea I was on the boat."

He got to the assembly point and was taken to the RSA, where he was given dry clothes before being taken home. "I was probably one of the first survivors home, in a police car," he says.
"I had a bit of shock. They put me to bed and I had a bit of a turn. I went to the doctor and he told me about my broken nose but after that it was back to normal. I went back to work after about a week."

Unbeknown to Tata, his colleague Dave McEwen had also jumped and washed up safe on the Eastbourne side. Eric Stretton made it ashore by lifeboat.

Tata kept his lifejacket. For some years it was on display at the Police Museum, where Tata would address groups of visiting youngsters. More recently it has been at the family home in Stokes Valley. "The lifejacket was a lifesaver," he says.

Tata pressed for Hoppy to be given an award for his heroics but was told that everyone had acted in an extraordinary way that day, so to single out an individual would be unfair.

He accepts that, but doubts that anyone did quite as much as Hoppy.

Tata left Police in 1975. "I decided I had a lucky break and that I would do something else," he says. "I went to work for my iwi, became secretary of the New Zealand Māori Council for 35 years. I had an opportunity to do something else and thought it would be more positive. Not that Police wasn't positive but there were a lot of gaps in Māori life that needed to be fixed."

He counts seven members of his whānau who serve or have served in Police, including a son, daughter and grandson.

"I've had a good life. I'm 83 and I've really made changes in my life."

Hoppy went back to work the day after the tragedy. In his 33-year Police career he achieved legendary status as a community officer in Naenae, in the Hutt Valley. He also served in Wellington's Armed Offenders Squad. In 1985 he received a Queens Service Medal for his police work and retired in 1989.

Both Tata and Hoppy have passed recently, two great men, tremendous examples of what good police are or should be.

The rescue operation was probably the biggest in New Zealandn history with 371 of the 629 police stationed in the Wellington District and at the Trentham Police Training School involved in the rescue of the passengers and crew of the Wahine.

The death toll at the end of the operation stood at 51 lives, with another dying within days and a further person dying of injuries many years later, a total of 53 lives lost on that stormy Wellington day in the harbour. There was also further loss of life due to tree falls and injuries from flying debris elsewhere in Wellington City.

Reference – Ten One Magazine April 2018

Wellington Storm

In the windswept rains on Te Atiawa's plains
In the land of the lower North Island
Where the clouds scud by in the foaming sky
And crash on the Rimataka highlands

The surge of the sea sweeps the surf to me
On the beach by the Hutt River mouth
I brace myself on the river mouth shelf
And confront the assault from the south

As the stormy sea thrusts the swells to me
From the base of the global sphere
The Antarctic bite of the cold wind's might
Cuts me deep as I'm standing here

Every sense is alivegrasp and strive
To capture the soul of the storm
And seize its strength right along the length
Of the beach in the Wellington morn

As the Ants in town all hunker down
Behind their double glazing
I'm out here in the storm swept air
With my eyes and senses blazing

Wildly awake, I stand there and take
The brute force of the southerly storm
But I feel no fear because I've been here
Long ago on a cold April morn

Fifty years ago in that cruel April blow
Nature's fury was fully unleashed
And fifty one died in the fierce raging tide
On the rocks near Pencarrow's beach.
On Barret's reef Wahine came to grief
In the heads of the harbour mouth
And rolled on its side in the seething tide
Destroyed by the storm from the south

I sat in the gloom of my puny classroom
As that roof flew off in the gale
And I stared in the eyes of the furious skies
So juvenile, frightened and frail

I learned on that day when a storm comes to play
That a terrible beauty abounds
And a raw tempest's might is a powerful sight
As a roof flies across the school grounds

That storm on its roll blew its way to my soul
And captured my heart with its splendour
Since then I delight in each storm's awesome might
As they transport me back to remember

There's no need for alarm, you'll not come to harm
As the storm tosses on in its play
And gives you a fright with its powerful might
As it welcomes you into the day

The thin autumn sun breaks this storm's sense of fun
As it did fifty years ago
And I laugh in its face, in one final embrace
As its powerful winds start to slow

The harbour then stills as the wind leaves the hills
As the latte sun ventures out
And the ants all smile down the town's golden mile
As they cautiously patter about

The storm is like life where we know joy and strife
And we only see beauty in one
But beauty is there in the hard times we bear
And we're poorer if we only love sun.

Composed by old school friend, life-long mate and talented poet Terry Jordan on 10 April 2018, 50th Anniversary of the Wahine Day Storm where 51 people lost their lives at sea with another two onshore.

Published with Terry's kind permission.

Sergeant Majors, Sub Inspectors and Detectives

Since 1886, when the nationalised New Zealand Police Force was formed out of the breakup of the New Zealand Constabulary Force into Defence and Police branches many rank names, classes and designations have come and gone. The only ranks that still exist today from 1886 are Constable, Sergeant and Inspector. The only designation that has stood the test of time is Detective, at one time a rank in the late 19th, early 20th century, but relegated to a designation, albeit with more pay and increased standing, since about the end of World War One.

In fact the above three ranks go back to the beginning of any form of policing in colonial New Zealand.

Holding rank in the police in the late 19th and early 20th century could be a temporary matter, very much at the will of politicians and Commissioners. In 1891 there were twelve Inspectors in the police, covering 12 police districts. It was decided by the then Minister that there were too many districts so, with a flourish of a pen, five districts disappeared, absorbed by the remaining seven. Five Inspectors were either retired or reduced in rank to Sergeant Major, just like that.

On 1 December 1894 Sub inspectors were re-introduced to replace the outgoing Sergeant Majors, undertake prosecution duties and relieve the clerical work of Inspectors. A Sub-Inspector rank existed previously but was disposed of as unnecessary.

By 1894 only three Sergeant Majors remained in the police, a rank held over from the New Zealand War days, the last one, William Mason, retiring in 1910. This last position over-lapped the establishment of a new upper NCO rank in 1906, Station Sergeants.

four being appointed, one each in the main centres to take the pressure off the Sub inspectors in those cities. The Station Sergeants took over prosecutions and paperwork, allowing the Sub-Inspectors more freedom for administration, supervision and training.

In 1904 Inspectors in the four main centres became City Inspectors. At this time there were no Superintendents. In 1911 the concept of a higher ranked NCO was recognised as needed throughout the colony so the rank of Senior Sergeant was established to help ease the pressure on Commissioned Officers in the districts. 12 very competent Sergeants were promoted and appointed.

The uniform ranks remained static for many years, with the Station Sergeants being converted to Senior Sergeants. Sub inspector remained as a rank until the 1950s when it was abolished with the establishment of Chief Inspector and Chief Superintendent ranks, existing and remaining Sub Inspectors becoming Inspectors.

The history of Detectives in the New Zealand police is interesting. There has always been some sort of Detective or plainclothes force in the police, very limited in numbers though. As late as the 1890s there were only 13 Detectives and oneChief Detective in the country. The detectives ranged from Detective 4th class, probably similar to Constable on Trial, to Detective 1st class, the Chief Detective. There was, back then, some rancour between the Detective branch and the uniform police. Much was made of the lack of supervision and discipline of detectives compared to uniform cops. Also Detectives got paid more, supposedly to fund informants and could receive reward monies provided by grateful insurance companies. The other side of the coin was that, with so few Detectives, they spent much of their time on the road investigating serious crime or undertaking surveillance or "special" duties with no time for a settled family life. The investigations being of a higher level and the ability to present evidence in the Supreme Court were also factors that marked Detectives apart from their uniform peers.

Surveillance soon became impossible as all Detectives were relatively well-known in the small society that was New Zealand then. New Constables were then used for such duties before becoming uniformed. This practice continued right into the 20th century.

In 1898 all the different classes in Constable, Detective and NCO ranks were abolished.

The designation of Chief Detective remained and gradually, after many arguments, a Commission of inquiry or two and some experimentation, became an established rank in the Detective Branch at the level of Senior Sergeant. At the beginning if a Chief Detective wanted to become Inspector he had to revert to a Uniform Senior Sergeant role before applying. This requirement soon disappeared and about 1920 a system was introduced that enabled promotion from one branch to the other for all aspiring NCOs and Officers in the Police.

As early as about 1918 a proposal was put forward by Detectives that the ranks of Detective Constable, Detective, Detective Sergeant and Detective Senior Sergeant be established to bring the Detective Branch in line with the Uniform police. This was not agreed to at the time but, as we know, did happen eventually, extending also into the officer ranks.
T
he Detective Branch was very much not its own master up until the 1920s with all Chief Detectives being under the supervision of uniform Inspectors in Districts. Detectives operating at a station run by uniform Sergeants were responsible to the Sergeants. Many disagreed with this, claiming that a Detective, by dint of service and experience, should be at least as equal as a uniform Sergeant. Many acrimonious episodes occurred as a result with some police carrying severe grudges against others for many years.

As the years went by, and usually following the numerous Commissions of Inquiry following bad things happening, the Detective branch increased dramatically, becoming the Criminal Investigation Branch in 1950 with its own rank structure up to, eventually, Detective Chief Superintendent. Movement between what was then the CIB and the Uniform Branch remained, upon promotion. Often CIB members would, over the course of their careers, move several times back into uniform for a while before resuming detective duties or perhaps choosing to remain in uniform, sharing their experience and knowledge of criminal investigation work with young staff. Some lucked out and once appointed a Constable on Trial, never wore uniform again in their careers despite numerous promotions.

In my time in the job there was still some acrimony towards the CIB by uniform staff. I did note at the time that the most critical Uniform Branch members were people who had not worked in the CIB, criticising from assumption rather than fact. Sadly some were of higher rank and should have known better.

Conversely, as a Detective Constable, Uniform Branch Sergeant and Uniform Branch Senior Sergeant on interchange I worked with some CIB members who regarded all uniformed staff as "wooden tops", incapable of catching a cold let alone a crim. Both viewpoints were cruel and very untrue.

As an NCO in smaller stations I relied on the local Detective or Detective Sergeant for his or her knowledge and experience when bad things happened. I also saw those same individuals get stuck in at pub fights, pulling cars over, locking up idiots for street offending just as I saw young uniform coppers locking up people for burglaries, thefts, cheque-offending and serious assaults, working under the guidance of either the Detective or a Uniform Branch member who had CIB experience.

Saner, more grounded people know both branches are necessary and movement between the branches essential to overcome these prejudices. This does not stop the good-natured banter between people in each branch and neither should it.

The last great change of ranking that I remember was the abolishing of Chief Inspectors and Chief Superintendents, replacing them with "levels" or class of Inspector and Superintendent, history repeating itself. Also the introduction of the rank of Assistant Commissioner in the 1980s has opened up a whole new layer of bureaucracy in the Police.

Lastly, on the subject of Chief Detectives, I did not know these existed until I was sent from Masterton to Wellington CIB as a Constable on Trial in 1975, told to report to the Chief Detective, Jim Crozier. I am not sure but I think Jim may have been one of the last Chief Detectives. He was, of course, an older experienced Detective Senior Sergeant but when I knew him he was the CIB equivalent of the Staff Senior Sergeant in Uniform Branch. A bit of a father-figure to young aspiring sleuths.

Sergeants

In the 8 or so years prior to my own promotion to Sergeant I probably had about a dozen Sergeants and Detective Sergeants as my supervisors in the Uniform Branch, the Criminal Investigation Branch and the Dog Section.

In my day the role of Sergeant was as a trainer, mentor and supervisor to Constables and Detectives. As we know, a Sergeant is pivotal to the career development or lack of for any young graduate from the Royal New Zealand Police College. Simply put, a Sergeant can make or break a new cop's career. The cop's own resilience is also a factor in being able to deal with different supervision styles displayed on occasions though. If a cop lacks resilience he or she will not stay long anyway.

Promotion from Constable to Sergeant is one of the bigger steps in a career for an aspiring leader in the Police. Some would say it is the biggest. It is the first time a cop is expected by virtue of his or her designation, to represent the views of the Police Administration to staff, to convey those views and to take responsibility for them being implemented. All this whilst still, mostly being an active street cop, investigator and crook catcher him or herself.

Most of my early Sergeants were great cops and supervisors, all with very different styles and personalities of course. They were all dedicated to helping me, by various means, fair and foul, to become a half decent cop myself. Some were like father or uncle figures due to their advanced age, over 45, and the fact some wore war medals on their chests. Others were like older brothers, sorry no sisters in my day, they were direct, supportive, humourous and, sometimes just bloody grumpy.

My first Sergeant was no example to follow, other than the ability to climb the ranks, which he did. He knew his job well but had some serious flaws, a predilection for turning over young couples in cars at night after watching them for a wee while, shining the torch on the unclad female a little too keenly. A tendency to smack mouthy females in the search room, I never saw him smack a male for some reason, not sure why. He was a religious clown and made a name for himself when the boys locked up two men for playing the beast with two backs in the Riverside carpark one night, only to find that one of the men was a minister in his church. The man was released into the custody of his bishop, to disappear overseas toute suite. His lover appeared before the beak the next day. His was an example of leadership I had no interest in following.

Another was a reasonably competent Sergeant in a very busy country station who spent his time on late shifts locked in the Senior Sergeant's office reading novels, asking not to be disturbed in the days when staffing consisted of one cop inside to look after prisoners, the counter and the 111 line, the other cop outside working alone or with a Maori Warden, MOT cop or a Civil Defence cop. The man was tired and possibly windy in a very busy and violent town.

Otherwise I was spoiled with brilliant leaders in all my roles before I became silly myself and made that leap into the junior rank of the unknowns. However there was one cop who was my sectional sergeant for quite a while. He was an example of the system not quite working the way it was intended to.

Jimmy was a quietly spoken, mild, seemingly shrinking little man. A thoroughly decent chap, honest as the day is long. He had a lovely family and a sense of humour once he got the joke which unfortunately was at his expense on many occasions. I liked him and respected him as a man as did most of our crew. He knew his law and procedure and could be quiet pernickety about some stuff. When on Court Section he would like the defendants to always do their top shirt buttons up before they appeared before His Worship the Magistrate. Some took exception to this enough for Jimmy to have to show his not inconsiderable physical strength, doing the button up for the defendant as well as blithely overcoming any physical resistance. This sometimes resulted in defendants appearing before His Worship choking and nodding due to lack of air as usually they were fat, smelly individuals. It became a dilemma for Jimmy when some defendants only had singlets. Jimmy would ask us to ring their family to get a shirt with a collar brought to the station prior to the hearing, like we did not have enough to do.

Prior to promotion Jimmy was a Constable in a small station on the West Coast. He was a clever little bugger academically so passed all his exams quickly. I know nothing of his service on the Coast but enough to say the leap to Sergeant was a huge bound for Jimmy that was never quite made.

In those days taking the piss, or in other words, friendly bullying of each other, was par for the course. Not allowed nowadays I am sure. Human Resources would be out guns blazing. They were simpler times where any personality defect; real or imagined, any faux pas, any small oops on the job was reason to have the piss taken. Jimmy was a crucible of all these so attracted more than his fair share of notice. Even the odd Senior Sergeant could not resist getting involved in some of the pranks played on Jimmy.

There was the toilet paper prank. A cunning detective, Tata Parata RIP, the station prankster, "obtained" some Department of Internal Affairs letterheads somehow. He then forged a letter from the Internal Affairs asking the Superintendent at Lower Hutt to undertake a survey of the number of toilet rolls used in the station. He either managed to get the boss, Bernie Kelly, to sign it or he forged the boss's signature, history is quiet on this, probably for a good reason.

A certain Senior Sergeant with a well-earned reputation as a prankster in his younger days, but now very circumspect and full of gravitas, as Seniors were in those days, minuted the report to Jimmy to complete the survey. Jimmy, being Jimmy, did not see through this but dutifully stalked the station for the next week asking everybody how much bog-roll they use daily at work, visiting all the toilets to do a stocktake at the beginning of the week and another at the end of the week. He was heard to ask one of our three WDs (policewomen) if he could inspect the girls WC which was in that forbidden land known as the Womens Division where no male was permitted. As a sensitive, somewhat shy country boy he was stuttering and stammering to the young cop who was starting to wonder what his motives were in wanting to accompany her alone into the inner sanctum of all that was virginal and good. The naughty Senior Sergeant heard this discourse in the corridor outside his office and thought bugger, we better stop this.

Jimmy was taken aside by the Senior Sergeant and the prankster from the first floor and had the prank explained. He laughed hesitatingly, thought it was funny. This made us all feel hmmm, well, Jimmy was a good humoured man, loyal to his staff, never swore or got stroppy, strong as an ox and liked to mix it on the street, he's alright. No more jokes were played on him. They were kept for more deserving cases.

The pressure of command got to Jimmy over the months I worked for him. He lost weight, went grey and became quite stooped. He was only a young man in his early thirties. Running a section of 7 or 8 Constables in a very busy city station was telling on him. We all liked him and did our best not to make his life difficult in front of the Seniors who were wondering what to do here.

As usually happens someone higher up decided to have it in for him. In those days you got promoted after you finished your exams and when you reached the top of the seniority list in any one year. This system and perhaps a well-meaning supervisor on the West Coast help Jimmy get his stripes. Jimmy was out of his depth in a city station and the powers that be should have known this. I left the station on transfer and a short while later I heard that Jimmy had decided to take his family back to the coast, applying for a Constable's role there. A course no doubt kindly suggested to him by the Inspector, a compassionate sort. I hope he enjoyed the rest of his career and has had a decent retirement in his home area.

Promotion is not for everybody. We all probably know examples of people who perhaps may have reached above their potential through no fault of their own. We also know many examples of colleagues who would have made wonderful bosses but decided that the Constable or Detective life was for them.

Senior Sergeants

The first time I ever knew there was such a creature as a Senior Sergeant in the New Zealand Police was the day I delivered, as a local boy straight from school, my luggage to the Police Training School at Trentham, the day before we fell in as a Cadet wing in Wellington. I was met by this genial old chap later revealed to be Senior Sergeant Ian Forsyth Croxford. He was in police uniform but had a crown on his arm, not a thing I had seen before. I knew about Sergeants and Inspectors, having been through the recruiting process and been interviewed by both. My father was with me and called Ian "Senior". I asked him later what that was about and learned about this unknown rank. It transpired that Ian Croxford was not going to show his genial side to us cadets, in fact the next day he acted like a martinet when we gathered in Holland House barracks in Wellington prior to visiting the Police Store, then in King Street, for our uniforms. He bellowed, strutted and told most of us to get our hair cut (again). I thought fuck, these Senior Sergeants are mean duces. Getting to know Ian in the following years he was indeed an amiable chap as a boss but we were not going to see that side of him as trainees.

I will not go too much into the rank structures of the Police in New Zealand in this article, saving that for another, more detailed, time. It is complicated and interesting. Suffice to say that there has nearly always been a senior NCO rank in our police going back to Armed Constabulary days. When the New Zealand Police fell out of the New Zealand Constabulary Force in 1886 the senior Non Commissioned rank of Sergeant Major was retained until the early 20th century, being abolished around the 1905 Commission of Inquiry as it smacked too much of drilling and military discipline. The rank insignia was four upside down chevrons on the right sleeve with a crown at the peak of the chevrons. Quite fetching if you are into that sort of thing. At about the same time or quite shortly, as the last Sergeant Majors were heading into retirement the appointment of four Station Sergeants in each of the main centres was authorised to help take the pressure off the then relatively new rank of Sub Inspector, a rank that would survive until after the Compton debacle in 1955 and another accompanying Commission of Inquiry.

Station Sergeants hefted the load of Prosecutions and Correspondence, leaving the Sub Inspectors free for administration duties. It was considered then and is still, I hope, a guiding thought now that Sergeants and senior NCO's, whatever name, were the backbone of the structure of supervision and control in the police, they were seen to be crucial in maintaining the discipline and performance of Constables. I cannot find any photos of the four Station Sergeants so am not sure what their rank insignia was. I know that some British Station Sergeants used to have a crown above their chevrons so maybe the New Zealand ones did to.

In 1911 the need for an established rank of a senior NCO outside of the four main centres was identified by the then Commissioner. This resulted in 16 suitable and highly competent Sergeants being promoted to the new rank of Senior Sergeant throughout the country. I assume the existing Station Sergeants also took the new rank. Thus the beginning of a rank that, 109 years later, despite recent attempts to downgrade or dispose of it, still exists in the New Zealand police. Initially the new Senior Sergeants wore four chevrons upside down on the right arm but in 1915 this was changed for the King George crown, similar to the blue Queen's crown still worn today on a shoulder slide but red in colour.

Getting back to cadet time, in our second year as Cadets, approaching graduation, the same Ian Croxford, our wing Chief Instructor, asked my class one day collectively where we saw ourselves in our future police careers. By then we had all been working in stations for over a year so knew the rank structure and the culture of a station, where everybody fitted in. A few said CIB, some said Inspector, quite a few just wanted to get to Constable first, and several, myself included, said Senior Sergeant. A view I was never to change. This fell out of a lecture given by Ian many months before about rank and structure. He was trying to explain the difference in duties between a Senior Sergeant and an Inspector. He, with some bluntness and perhaps exasperation said " Senior Sergeants are kings of the shit, Inspectors are shit of the kings" looking directly at all of us as he liked to do. Never forgot that, made sense to me.

Senior Sergeants, by their very nature, are usually distant souls, not to be annoyed or upset by silly Constables. As a young cop all my Seniors were older men, medals galore, quiet, measured, older than my father, distant but in a friendly way mostly. All were good coppers and most had a sense of humour. They usually stayed inside the station, letting the Sergeants run the streets as they should. Rarely would they go out, only if there was a reason such as a demonstration, a riot, disaster, big stuff, where an Inspector needs a senior person on the ground.

As I, like most young police, grew into the job, the Senior Sergeants became younger, still distant and measured, hopefully still good coppers, although I did begin to wonder at times. As a new young Sergeant I then had a new relationship with the Senior Sergeants at my station, staying on in the same station upon promotion. They became friendlier but also had far higher expectations of me. They confided in me matters that I would never, as a Constable, be privy too, bestowing on me the responsibility of keeping my mouth shut as well. They even allowed me to do their job on occasions. Most had wide police experience in both Uniform and CIB and great networks in the job because of this. Senior Sergeants teach cops and Sergeants almost by osmosis. They are just there in the background, guiding, suggesting, steering matters. Their relationship with Inspectors and above can be interesting.

Morning meetings or "prayers" with the District Commander in large stations always show this off with the District Commander, at least a Superinetendent, the Area Commander who is an Inspector or in my day, Chief Inspector, one or two other Inspectors, the Detective Senior Sergeant, the Staff Senior Sergeant and the duty Senior Sergeant. A humble Uniform Branch Sergeant and a Detective Sergeant, both usually in charge of day shifts at the time, would sit quietly in the corner. The boss runs the District, the Area Commander runs the town and station but the Senior Sergeants really run the day to day operations of a busy station. Decisions were never made without input from the Seniors who actually knew the incidents, the cops involved, and the reasons for some issues that arose. They are the eyes and ears of the administration. Decent officers know this, having been there themselves, and use the Seniors properly. Rarely some plain talking happens.

Senior Sergeants also, in many district stations in my time, undertook Police Complaints Authority Inquiries, there usually being simply too many for an Inspector or Chief Inspector to do on his or her own. These ranged from trivial to serious, resulting in the normal outcomes expected, exonerations, warnings, charging and firing. We were strongly supervised by the Authority which, overall, was a better, fairer system than prior to the Authority being established in my experience.

Senior Sergeants of either branch in my time had different relationships with their Sergeants. There were good, average and poor Sergeants and it was the Senior's job to manage these first line supervisors. A section or squad of hard working coppers stands or falls on the sectional or squad Sergeant's personality, ability and leadership skills. This is mostly never an issue but expectations had to be set early in a new Sergeant's relationship with a Senior Sergeant. Being human, we would normally remain mates and just get on with it, both knowing and supporting each other's strengths and weaknesses. Sometimes not. That's the job.

Senior Sergeants ran operations, Search and Rescue, Armed Offenders incidents, riots, homicides and other serious crime inquiries etc. They all have command knowledge and experience, organisation charts, logistics, maps, chalk boards, overhead projectors, all good stuff. Good Inspectors let the Seniors get on with it, hanging in the background with support and advice unless needed. I remember it being a big job at times.

I was very proud to be a Senior Sergeant for a few years in a busy provincial station. I achieved my ambition expressed as a Cadet and never regretted it. I worked with some brilliant Officers and Sergeants as a Senior Sergeant, whilst still learning from both. Like all busy NCOs I had bad times, one was losing a cop on my watch, a mate, then doing the body recovery, mortuary procedure, the coronial inquiry and the actual inquiry into the incident.

"What has been seen cannot be unseen, what has been learned cannot be unknown. You cannot change the past, but you can learn from it. You can grow from it. You can be made stronger. You can use that strength to change your life, to change your future." – C.A Woolf, American author.

.

Commissioned Officers of Police

The New Zealand Police has about 8 ranks or designations from Constable to Senior Sergeant if you include Senior Constable, Dog Handler, Senior Detective, Detective, Detective Sergeant, Sergeant and Detective Senior Sergeant. The only actual ranks are Constable, Sergeant and Senior Sergeant, the rest are designations based on service, training and qualification.

Once a person obtains promotion to Inspector, the lowest rank for Commissioned Officers in the New Zealand Police, he or she faces a multitude of ranks and positions to aspire to, ending with the top job, Commissioner of Police. In my day, no matter what rank a cop held from the most junior Probationary Constable to the Commissioner, they were all legally sworn as Constables under the 1958 Police Act. This was the cause for some fun over the years with cops and sergeants applying for the Commissioner's job on occasions as applications were invited from all sworn Constables. Things may now be different of course. Everything is.

Having never aspired to or been really that interested in becoming an Inspector, despite sitting the exams for the fun of it, being a bit of a nerdy swot, I never really worked out how the various Officer ranks worked or what one had to do to get ahead as the promotion exam system then stopped at Inspector. What follows is my insight as a cop who worked with and for many Commissioned Officers over the years from Cadet to Senior Sergeant.

To aspire to high command in the Police is a noble but challenging ambition. With the high command and its perks and rank comes increasing responsibility and pressure. All police in New Zealand start their careers as Constables; there is no direct-entry officer scheme here despite occasional papers supporting this.

The one good thing about this is that most high-ranking officers have had sound police experience through every rank with many in both the Criminal Investigation Branch and Uniform Branch. They are seasoned cops by the time they become new Inspectors, well that is the aim and the hope.

The downside to this system is that it is very slow for the ambitious young cop who wants to get to the top as soon as possible. All Commissioned Officers are different, as is everybody, but the two things that they all need to have in spades is integrity and honesty. I have served with some wonderful bosses, natural leaders and great managers. Some have had their funny wee ways, annoying at times, but they were good at their jobs, a credit to the promotion system and the training scheme offered to aspiring Inspectors.

I have served with a few wombles, totalling out of their depth in the rank, a fact everyone knows and puts up with until they either get promoted again and moved on, usually to Police National HQ to while their time away on little pointless projects until they can retire with some dignity, a favourite ploy with public service administration in the old days, or realise themselves they are working at a level above their competence and leave, unfortunately, usually the first option because coming with the incompetence is sometimes a lack of insight into their own abilities or lack of.

This was hugely obvious during the 1981 Springbok Tour when Police National Headquarters was emptied out of Commissioned Officers to take field command roles around the country. Us Wellington cops would meet our new Commanders, none of whom we knew, other than they were from HQ. Some were great bosses, got things done, lead from the front, backed their crew, we could not wish for more. Others were hopeless, dithering idiots having to be prompted by Senior Sergeants or Sergeants on what tactics to use, completely out of their depth and very unhappy. One even took off in his car and left us to it on the Wellington Motorway at Horokiwi, Leaving the second In Charge, a Senior Sergeant, to sort out the arrest of over 50 demos. He was never seen again. I guess the Senior sergeant advised the higher-ups but we never heard what happened. Desertion under fire!!

As a street cop for most of my service, apart from lengthy periods as a prosecutor, I had reason to meet with Inspectors, Chief Inspectors and Superintendents on a semi-regular basis to help them understand my point of view about certain allegations being made against me or mine. Sometimes of course I would bluntly decline such meetings due to not wanting to embarrass the interviewing officer with my frank and open honesty. I remember a small altercation I was involved in with the Black Power in Foxton in the 1980s. Well, it wasn't small, but anyway. Suffice to say blood was shed, a police station burned down and all our police vehicles had their tyres slashed. The Black Power lost the fight of course. An inquiry started, as they tend to do after such affrays, and charges were recommended, people were worried, perhaps with good reason, some roles were lost but no one got kicked out of the police and most of us got a good arse-kicking from the Regional Commander of Region 4. Manawatu/Whanganui/New Plymouth, Assistant Commissioner Stuart McEwen.

During the course of the inquiry I was at the Police College on one of my regular jaunts there for some advanced course or other, some misguided soul at Police National Headquarters kept sending me to the College in the hope I might begin to, one day, take the job seriously, but that's another story. The Officer in Charge of the Inquiry, an affable chap, Detective Inspector who became a Mayor, a nice guy, rang and asked me to attend an interview with him later in the day after class at the college. He was driving down from Palmerston North that afternoon. I explained to him that, as much as I would enjoy his company, I cannot attend the interview and will not answer any of his questions. He stuttered and stammered a wee bit, not expecting this response from good old Ratts. I learnt very early on as a young Sergeant, to my great cost, never, ever, be interviewed in an inquiry. If they have enough they will charge me, why should I help.

Class finishes and the Duty Constable turns up asking for me, saying Detective Inspector so and so is here to see me. I race down to the college HQ, warmly greeted the inspector, declined his kind offer of an interview and invited him for a beer at the bar. He declined my invite saying he had driven all the way from Palmerston North to see me. I then reminded him of our conversation, reiterating that I will not be interviewed. Charge me or whatever but I am off for a wet. It had been a long hard day in class. He was quite upset and I actually felt sorry for him as he is a nice guy and was only doing his job. But I also knew that he, being a cunning detective of some note, would know most of the answers to his questions before asking me. I did not need to confirm or prove anything.

I also invited him to dinner but he declined saying he better head home. Everyone knew the rules but everyone has to do their jobs in internal inquiries. Later as a Senior Sergeant I would be on the opposite side of the fence with Constables and Sergeants telling me the same thing when conducting Police Complaint Authority inquiries. No worries.

There have been times when I and others have had the benefit of guidance and mentoring from older Commissioned Officers, vastly experienced men who knew human nature and knew how the job worked. Those officers received my undying loyalty as a result, they could have dealt with various issues much differently. There were some Commissioned Officers who were zealous in their duties and liked to keep a personal record of the cops they had charged or fired. I was very lucky that I never had the misfortune to work for any of these types. Some fine men and women lost their careers because of a lack of understanding, empathy and some personal prejudice displayed by certain officers towards junior staff. I totally respect and admire a man or woman who decides to take the leap into an Inspector's role. It only gets tougher and the load heavier. Many are cut out for high command but some are not and fall by the wayside. Some, like me, recognised that the load was not worth the personal cost to family and health and stayed at the street end of the job all our service. I have many mates who are ex Commissioned Officers and they are, to a man and woman, fine people and were fine leaders and managers. Many you could see it in them as young cadets or recruits, but most developed later.

The most embarrassing moment in my career was as a young probationary Constable sitting, drinking beer in the bar at Lower Hutt police station with a couple of grey-haired old gentlemen drinking gins, not uniformed, looking like old grandads. Myself and a couple of other 19 year old "experts" were going on about "Fishhead" Commissioned Officers being a waste of space, never doing any police work yah-de-yah. These old chaps were sitting there smiling; the Wellington District Commander, a Chief Superintendent, and his second in charge, a Superintendent, on a station visit, waiting in the bar for a drink with our bosses Superintendent Bernie Kelly and Inspector Peter Goodyear. One of us went to the bar for his shout and one of the older cops present at the bar asked did we know who we were talking to. My mate came back, dropped us our beers and went to the leaner behind these old guys, indicating for us to follow. He told us who they were. I then tried to find a hole in the floor to swallow me. I could never look these two seemingly kindly old gents in the eye again.

How Times Have Changed – "Muzz" – A Gay Cop

My name is Muzz and for the period 1971 to 1985, I served with the New Zealand Police in a number of North Island stations.

I loved my job and performed my duties to the best of my ability and always enjoyed the camaraderie and all for one, one for all attitude that is important in a law enforcement service. There were good times, there were bad times. I saw things that will stay with me forever but I was very fortunate that the shocking sights I did see from time to time had no long term affect on me as it sadly does with some of the 'Blue Family.' I never backed away from the more unpleasant jobs and felt proud and contented when I was able to be part of any task that ended satisfactorily with the upholding of law and order as the paramount goal and result. There was one thing that set me apart from the large majority of my fellow workmates, I was homosexual but due to the laws of the time, very 'closeted.' Before I continue with my story, a little history lesson of how things evolved here in New Zealand. Same-sex relationships and activities are reported to have been accepted amongst pre-colonial Maori society. There were no legal or social punishments for engaging in same-sex sexual activity. Male homosexual intercourse was criminalised when New Zealand became part of the British Empire in 1840. In 1893 the law in New Zealand was broadened to outlaw any sexual activity between men. Penalties included life imprisonment, hard labour and flogging. Sex between women has never been criminalised in New Zealand.

During my time with the New Zealand Police, Sections 141 and 142 of the Crimes Act 1961 (since repealed) were the main crimes related to male same-sex activity. Both sections carried imprisonment penalties which made men like myself criminals in the eye of the law if we chose to partake of course! The hypocrisy of being a law enforcement officer on one hand and a 'criminal' on the other, troubled me greatly and drove me further into the 'closet.' It wasn't until the embattled and bitter campaign in the 1980s and the Homosexual Law Reform Act1986 moved by Labour MP Fran Wilde, that things started to improve. The Act was narrowly passed thus legalising homosexual acts in New Zealand between consenting males 16 years and over.

The Human Rights Act Amendment not allowing discrimination against sexual orientation etc, came in later years. All this was after I resigned but no doubt affected LGBT staff making it a little easier as the years went by.

And now for my story ……..

I was born into a working class family in Auckland and have memories of caring and loving parents who worked hard to give my siblings and I the best life possible in the 1950s. From a very early age and from as far back as I can remember, I knew there was something different with me with regards to my sexuality and how I felt. At school I did all the 'boy things' with playing sport etc but never felt overly attracted to girls. It worried me a little as being the only male child, I was no doubt being looked at to carry on the family name and all that goes with it. To the critics who claim that sexual orientation (not preference!!) is something learned or happens after being indecently assaulted as a child, I can openly say that this is not true on either count for me and I believe that it is something we are born with.

I was not a brilliant student at school and was probably placed in the middle of the class with my studies. I actually got to dislike school more and more as I grew older and my parents allowed me to leave the day I turned 15 to pursue a scholarship course. When a Police recruiting campaign was going on in the

1970 period, I decided that it was a career that I would enjoy and the training and service would toughen me up a bit. I had missed out on the Compulsory Military Training ballot that was in force at the time, but wouldn't have minded doing the training as I saw it as helping to 'make a man' out of me. In hindsight I now wonder if my sexuality was always in the back of my mind and I wanted to do something that would make me like all the other guys. A Police career however was always something I felt I could handle and it would give me a satisfying, stable and secure work future. The matter of male same sex activities being a crime at the time was always something on my mind so I tried to convince myself that I was bisexual and everything would be OK.

I applied to join the NZ Police during 1970 and got accepted for the 1971 January to April Recruit Wing at the old Police Training School at Trentham near Wellington. During the latter part of the recruitment process, I was interviewed by a Superintendent of Police at Auckland Central Police Station. I remember the last question he asked me was how my parents felt about me wanting to join the Police. I replied that they thought it would mature and make a man out of me and be a good career. He agreed with that view and shortly after I was advised I had been accepted for training.

In January 1971 at the age of 20 I boarded the overnight Wellington express along with a number of other Auckland area recruits and we were off with a certain amount of trepidation as to what awaited us.

My school education, or lack of it, was one thing that I worried about with the amount of study and exams to pass that I knew lay ahead. Trentham was by no means a palace with each of the three recruit sections in old military accommodation huts with two in a room and communal ablution blocks. I thrived on the training and really enjoyed the PE and unarmed combat part of it led by the very well respected and hard task master Senior Sergeant

Jimmy Page (RIP.) I found the classroom lessons and night time study difficult but put my head down and worked hard. During this period of time there had been isolated incidents of same sex activities discovered amongst male trainees with the inevitable dismissals, so I put my feelings further to the back of my mind and just worked hard. I graduated about middle of my wing and it was a very proud day indeed to parade in front of my family on graduation day. In the three months spent at Trentham, I had gone from a somewhat shy thin (but fit) 11 and a bit stone weight, to a more confident 12 stone plus sworn Police Constable. I was proud of what I had achieved and even though Trentham Camp was a hard place to be in, I missed it and the great friendships formed. It was indeed sad saying good bye but we all looked ahead to what awaited us in our allotted Stations.

Being single and transferred from Trentham back to my home area of Auckland, the normal living arrangements were in barracks. I was sent to Otahuhu so was allowed to live at my home. Otahuhu was a great grounding station for a new young Constable and a bit like being thrown in the deep end but I learnt fast and was lucky to get jobs and experiences that my fellow wing mates did not get in the bigger stations. I also worked with a great section of staff, some with not much more service than me but with a heap of experience that they willingly shared. I remember attending a multiple fatal motor accident on the Southern Motorway not long after arriving at Otahuhu. A fellow Constable from Auckland Central who I had been with at Trentham was also there and when we compared notes of what we had done, I was surprised how much more experience and job variety I had from working in a smaller station.

As time went on in the early stages of my career, I realised that homophobia was quite rampant in the job and with male same sex activities still being illegal, the phobia probably wasn't overly surprising amongst law enforcement staff. The sad part of this was that I also had a certain amount of homophobia engrained in me mainly due to wanting to carry on as a Police Constable and also being in a form of denial by putting my feelings down to being bisexual. 'Homo' jokes were common and sadly I sat and laughed at the best (or worst) of them. Looking back now, I have feelings of shame and regret, but I did what I did in the early days to survive in the job and also to hide what would later come out as my true feelings.

Later in 1970, I met a lovely young lady who caught my eye at a gathering one night. My experiences with women, mainly due to my hidden feelings, had been minimal up to this stage. I saw this young lady as someone who I could fall in love with and hopefully one day marry. During a period of her planned OE for 2 years, we kept in touch and carried on with our relationship upon her return to New Zealand. I was still enjoying being a Police Constable but the deeply hidden closeted feelings did surface at times and were quickly subdued and pushed to the back of my mind again. We married a couple of years after she returned from her OE. At this stage I must point out that I never used this as a shield or 'cover' and I did really love her but in hindsight not the sort of love to keep a healthy marriage going. We were married for about 8 years during which a son was born. My son and I met again when he was much older and I am proud and thankful to still have contact with him and his family.

The pride of what he has achieved in his life pleases me greatly and I reckon he got his brains from his Mum more than me! As I grew older I found my closeted feelings becoming stronger and struggled with them. At the same time hiding my feelings in a macho and somewhat homophobic Police Department was proving to be a huge struggle. I loved and respected my wife (and all these years later still do to a certain extent) but finally realised I was doing both of us no favours with how I felt. Our break-up was very difficult and I know I hurt many people, my dear wife being the one most hurt. It is something I have never been proud of and I will probably never totally forgive myself for what I did.

At the time of the marriage split, we were living and working up north. Being on my own with all the other confusion and feelings in my mind, I decided a transfer back to the big smoke of Auckland would be a good idea. At the time I was receiving counselling in Auckland so the transfer amongst other things would make these sessions closer and easier. The counselling was top secret as had it been known about in the job, my future in the Police would have ended. Thankfully today this type of scenario has changed for the better. The only way to get a transfer was to do it with someone in Auckland who wanted to swap with me. I arranged this and transferred back to Auckland and to, yes you guessed it, Otahuhu!! With exams and the service I had, I was made up to an Acting Sergeant on a section of young keen Constables.

My time at Otahuhu was difficult but I did my best and as time went on I realised that moving back to the big smoke was probably not my best decision and that I would not be in the job much longer. I enjoyed the Auckland gay social scene and would never have done anything to embarrass the job, but the possibility of being spotted in a gay night club etc was always on the cards. At the time fellow gay officers were being 'outed' and dismissed from the job so all of this just added to the pressure and stress I was under.

A vacancy came up for a Constable at Auckland Airport and I was lucky enough to get the position. The pressures of the job weren't as much at the airport but I still could not enjoy my social life and being 'me'. Around this time, homosexual law reform was in full swing and carried with it more publicity for the 'community'. TV cameras and reporters were often at gay bars and clubs so my chances of being spotted increased. I have fond memories of a gay bar in the old Alex pub that was operated by Elaine Timperley. Elaine knew I was in the Police – I actually had the nick name of

'Blue Boy' with a few of the regulars! – so she would warn me if the cameras were coming into the bar. I would make myself scarce until the cameras and reporters left.

What was a little bit ironical at the time was that with female same sex activities not being illegal, a few lesbian Police staff I knew were able to be out and proud in front of the cameras while I was away hiding somewhere. This was certainly not the way I wished to live my life anymore so leaving the job, which I really did not want to do, became the only option for me. I resigned in 1985 feeling rather bitter that I felt the need to. I felt it was my only choice with the risk of being found out, probably charged and dismissed and bringing further shame to my family being something I did not want to do.

At the time of the law reform battle, a few Government MPs showed their true colours and the things they were saying became hateful to say the least. I am not one to speak ill of the dead, but one of the biggest objectors was National MP Norman Jones. At one of the meetings attended by those for and against the proposed Bill, Jones, referring to a large group of supporters said – "Turn around and look at them ….. gaze upon them ….. you're looking into Hades ….. don't look too long ….. you might catch AIDS." This was the type of hatred that existed at the time and the work of the supporters of the Bill is something to be admired with the discord they were facing.

In conclusion, I will always be thankful to the few friends in the Police (they know who they are) who knew where I was 'at' and were there for me at the time. You became my rocks when I needed a bit of support and friends I knew I could talk to in confidence. Without you, the journey would have been so much harder.

The Police Department of today has changed since my time. Even though I left feeling bitter, I still have enormous respect and support for the difficult job they do in this modern diverse world. The many staff from different ethnicities, diverse backgrounds – LGBT etc – is great to see. Let's carry this on and be safe out there!

Some Memories and Musings of a Retired Cop
Articles Originally Written for Serving and Ex-Police

Prime Ministers I have Met as a Personal Protection Officer, Dog Handler and Father

There are times as a cop that one gets to work with the great and the good, usually looking after them. I looked after three Prime Ministers and a Governor General at various times and places in my time with the Police. In those far off safe days New Zealand Prime Ministers did not have full time personal bodyguards and security teams as they do now. They were usually allocated an Inspector, Senior Sergeant or Sergeant as their Personal Protection Officer as and when needed when out of Wellington. In the provincial areas most of the allocated staff were members of the Armed Offenders Squad.

At Wellington events or major national or international events the Diplomatic Protection Squad would allocate staff to guard the Prime Minister and any other VIP involved.

There has always been various threats made against Prime Ministers from disaffected people, pressure groups and nutters. These were all investigated by the CIB back in the day to assess the level of threat and locate the offender.

Sir Robert David Muldoon was Prime Minister of New Zealand from 1975 to 1984. Muldoon did not feel the need to be reasonable with many people and this resulted in him receiving more than his share of threats. This was like water off a duck's back to him but made a lot of work for the Police. From 1976 to 1979 I operated Dyna, the Wellington Explosive and Firearm Detector dog, one of the first three such dogs trained in New Zealand. We worked as part of the security team for Muldoon all over New Zealand. My personal contact with Muldoon was minimal and frosty to say the least. We would often have to search and clear the Prime Minister's residence, Vogel House, in Lower Hutt prior to functions and dinners so Muldoon got used to the sight of Dyna and I in the grounds of the house or in the house itself. He always pointedly ignored us if he was in the grounds. However his wife Thea loved dogs and I would occasionally take Dyna upstairs to the Prime Minister's personal flat in the building for Mrs Muldoon to catch up with Dyna, who got spoiled with biscuits or cakes.

I never got anything, just stood in the corner of the room with Muldoon glowering at me if he was present. After about five minutes we would leave, promising to call again and Muldoon would get back to his reading or TV. I could never work out why such a nice lady as Mrs Muldoon was married to such a pig of a man.

While they were living at Vogel House the safety of the Prime Minister and his wife were the responsibility of Lower Hutt Police and the Diplomatic Protection Squad. The house was connected directly to the Lower Hutt police station by raid alarm. If the PM had a problem he need only push the alarm and armed police would descend within minutes. If Muldoon had spent a bit too long in Bellamy's he would occasionally like to have a little fun at the expense of the on-duty staff. He would set the alarm off after getting home from the pub, probably driving himself, and then stand in the porch timing the arrival of the first armed patrol. Upon their arrival he would express his pleasure or otherwise, cackle that weird laugh and walk through the door, closing it behind him, leaving the police fuming outside.

Muldoon had his own traffic rules as well. In the late 1970s he self-drove many days from Vogel House to Parliament and return, usually with a marked police patrol tailing him. Speed limits did not seem to apply to him and he would delight in trying to shake the police car on the motorway. A bit of a character.

Sir Keith Holyoake was one of New Zealand's longest-serving Prime Ministers. From 1977 to 1980, upon his retirement from politics he was appointed Governor- General of New Zealand. One of the regular ports of call for Dyna and I was Government House, usually as part of a security team prior to special functions, to clear the house. Sir Keith was an amiable soul and very friendly towards the dog. He was, by then, an elderly gent, so liked to retire early most evenings. Dyna and I were required to search the huge building the night before some function. By the time we got there His Excellency was abed. No worries, the Aide de Comp ushered the dog and I into the boss's bedroom while he was in bed much to the delight of the old chap. We did a quick search and out of there.

In about 1985 the police realised that more Personal Protection Officers needed to be trained around the country in the provinces and big cities to help take the load off a very busy Diplomatic Protection Squad. Up until then there was no formal training programme for police who undertook personal protection work other than, perhaps, Armed Offenders Squad training which whilst very good, was not focused on protecting dignitaries. As a Sergeant I attended one of the first courses at the police college in 1985 with Constable Colin "Ox" Wightman as representatives of the Whanganui police district. We spent a few weeks range shooting with short-barrelled large-handled Smith & Wesson six shot revolvers issued specifically for PPO work in the provinces. We also learned basic motorcade drills and debussing tactics, all good Boys Own cowboy stuff. Our instructors were DPS staff, Armed Offender Squad staff and one or two military staff. Upon returning to our districts we were then to be the PPOs for incoming dignitaries. Prime Ministers usually liked to visit provinces back then in a reasonably low key way either flying or coming by car with a Public Service driver and a PA for company. They would be booked into the flashest pub in town and would be met by two local PPOs who would stay by their sides for the entire visit, usually a day or just overnight but sometimes several days.

PPOs were required to be in plainclothes, suit and tie and were armed with the short barrelled Smith & Wesson pistol, carried either in a Bianchi shoulder holster or in a kidney holster on the hip. The pistols had large grips so were little different in size and bulk to the issue .357 Magnum Smith & Wesson pistols issued to AOS back then. I would normally carry the Magnum, my personal weapon, on these jaunts. We also had personal radios and handcuffs of course and travelled in a plain CIB car.

In late 1985 Prime Minister David Lange visited Whanganui with our local MP Russell Marshall and a flunky or two. Ox and I were briefed by the District Commander and set forth. We met Mr Lange at the Grand Hotel in Whanganui. As we arrived he came out of his room with a large platter of sandwiches and savouries, thrust this into Ox's hands and said, "you two eat them, I'm trying to lose weight". We did our best at our little station outside his door. He also gave us tea or coffee. I was thinking, this guy is the PM, what a nice guy. All the time he was talking, joking with Marshall and their staff, dictating letters and generally having the time of his life. Ox and I spent two days with Mr Lange and his party. There was little or no threat against this kindly man and Whanganui was, in those days, a safe Labour seat. When he had time on his hands Mr Lange liked to look around the district so Ox and I acted as his guides, showing him around the place, meeting locals and helping him get to appointments on time as he did like to chat to everyone. He kept very long hours so we did too, no booze but plenty of local party people he had to spend time with. Ox and I ate like kings and were entertained non-stop for the two days the PM was in Whanganui by his wit and sense of fun. He thanked us effusively when he left and we both got "attaboys" from the boss within a week or so. I always liked the guy, such a talented man who died too soon.

A few years later David Lange tossed in the Prime Minister's job due to ructions within the Labour Party and Sir Geoffrey Palmer replaced him as Prime Minister from August 1989 until September 1990 when Labour left office. Sir Geoffrey arrived in Whanganui late one evening without any great fanfare, staying at the Grand Hotel where Constable Robin Dwane and myself met him at breakfast the following morning. He promptly ordered us to sit down and have breakfast with him, which we did. We had a great conversation with this learned, considerate man. He really seemed interested in what we were doing. Rob and I spent a happy day with Sir Geoffrey and his driver visiting various places around town before they departed back to Wellington mid-afternoon. A very low-key prearranged visit with hardly anybody knowing he was in town. A real gentleman.

I never had any more to do with serving Prime Ministers after this, promotion taking me away from this form of hands-on policing.

In 1999 Helen Clark became Prime Minister of New Zealand. The first elected female Prime Minister. This was the same year our youngest, Luke, joined the New Zealand Army. Helen Clark has a strong soft spot for military personnel. In the years from 1999 onwards New Zealand has sent thousands of young military personnel overseas to various trouble sports, East Timor, Iraq and Afghanistan being the main places. New Zealand's military had very strong and defined riding instructions from Helen Clark's government. She wanted these young people to all safely come home, most did thankfully. Ms Clark made it her mission, if in New Zealand, to personally either farewell or greet military contingents leaving or returning to New Zealand. She also wanted to meet the loved ones o f these returned people, the wives, husbands, mothers and fathers.

Luke spent his share of time in the military overseas so we were always saying goodbye or meeting him when he came home after months away. A very stressful time for parents. One of Luke's last deployments was to Basra in Iraq, a very bad place then. New Zealand military shared the British base in that city. He was due to fly in with his contingent at about 2.00 a.m. one morning at Ohakea Air Force Base. We drove down to meet him and welcome him home. When we got there we were met by Helen Clark. We were in this huge hangar with hundreds of other anxious relatives awaiting their loved ones and the PM was working the huge room, spending time with every family group. She was accompanied by a young female Naval Officer and her consideration to us was genuine and deeply felt. What Prime Minister would get up in the middle of the night, travel 140 kms to an air force base in the middle of nowhere to meet a whole bunch of strangers awaiting their loved ones, then spend a good hour or two in this huge hangar socialising with everyone?

Yes, I know that they are politicians, but they are also people too with feelings and needs.

Trentham

In 1914 Hut 211 was built at Trentham Army Camp as temporary accommodation for troops training for World War 1. In January 1970 me and 81 mates moved into Huts 211 and 210, then part of the Trentham Police Training School. We were allocated a cubicle to every three guys, the cubicles being about the size of an average single bedroom in a 1960s house, very small. On one wall were two bunks and on the opposite wall the third. There were three lowboys in a row in between that probably arrived by horse and cart when the place was built. There were only two wardrobes, the third being down the corridor. Opposite, across the very narrow passage was a mirror of our cubicle with three other 17 year old cadets trying to fit in.

This was our living quarters until August 1970 when the previous cadet wing graduated. We were then able to move into two man bedrooms which were slightly larger.

Very intimate was the living in those days. No privacy whatsoever.

We were also introduced to the Immigration Hostel dining room run by Whites Caterers otherwise known as Luigi's. After 17 years of being looked after by our dear mums and fed good wholesome food, and plenty of it we were shocked to be introduced to Luigi's menu. He used to cater out to the community so every Monday we would get the leftovers from the weekends weddings and socials in the Hutt Valley. The fried rice had weevils in it, the roast meat had begun to turn green, the mince bore no real resemblance to the mince we ate at home. The vegetables were either strained to puree or before the stage of al dente. Breakfast was a real treat. The toast lady, an older woman who had an unfortunate and itchy facial skin condition which earned her the nickname of "old turkey buzzard" from an unkind few, used to use her hands to put the toast on our plates. No tongs or hair nets in those days.

It was rumoured that Luigi used to make the mince while smoking over the vat but I never saw this. The only food that was reasonably safe to eat was sausages, not much could be done to these other than wondering where the cooks fingers had been. Pint bottles of milk were also popular as they were sealed.

Luigi was there for the money. In those days he would feed several hundred at a sitting. most of Police school, the Ministry Of Transport trainee Traffic Officers, the Maori Trade Training guys and the various block apprentice courses who all lived in our area of the camp. The food was abysmal and complaints just fell on deaf ears.

I was there one day when an entire recruit wing went through, picked up their plates and emptied them straight into the slop bins, walking out.

There were two other messes in Trentham, the Post Office Accommodation Block mess where I was lucky to spend two terms, slightly better fare but very average still, and the Army mess which my section missed out on due to some rambunctious behavior one weekend. The penalty for these high-jinks was a third term at Luigi's.

Advanced courses I attended all ate at Luigi's so this was our life as young and not so young cops from 1956 to 1981 when the new college opened in Porirua.

I was on the first Sergeants course at Porirua in early 1981, along with several other courses put together to form the guard of honour for the opening of the college by his Royal Smallness Prince Charles. I could not believe the food we were served, it was like staying in a five star hotel. We were allowed a choice of meats, seconds, there was fruit, pasta, juices. At about this time I decided that I would become a serious course attender. Coming home from courses at the College was a reason to get out running again as the weight just slipped on.

The Physical Training Instructors, in some frustration, approached the ex-military cooks and asked if they could moderate the diets of the recruits as the PTI's wanted weight kept down. The boss cook, probably a crusty old Army Warrant Officer, told the PTI staff that he does not tell them how to run a gym, so do not try to tell him how to run a dining room!! The good old days.

Avalon Gaming Raid

Older people may remember gaming raids in the good old days. New Zealand has a long history of illegal gambling amongst all levels of society. I only ever got involved in one such raid as a cop but it was quite memorable. There has always been illegal gaming houses in New Zealand going back to the pioneer days. In 1976, whilst in the CIB in Wellington Central, I was part of a huge group of Police who raided a den in Lower Hutt one fine summers evening. Information had been received that tickets were being sold to an illegal gaming evening at the Mabey Road Hall, in Avalon, by Barry Keith Davis and associates. Davis was a serious and up and coming criminal who associated with some of the big boys of the criminal underworld in the 1970s and 80s in Wellington. I knew Barry well, having grown up near him and, as our mothers were childhood friends, associating with his family quite a bit when I was a child. He was a tough bastard so I knew we would be in for some fun and games when we busted the hall.

The vice squad had put a "special" into the place, the redoubtable Detective Max To'o. We based ourselves at the Lower Hutt station to await the word from Max. Upon hearing things were going well at the hall we hot footed up to Avalon to knock the place over. We get there and were seen coming of course. The doors were locked on us, we knew this was likely. We had a team of guys tasked with breaking the door in so they got to work with axes etc. Unbeknown to them the doors opened outwards and Max was inside trying to unlock and open them for us. Each time the guys hit the doors they shut again.

Anyway, long story short, we got in once the boys worked the door thing out. There was a fair number of us and the hall was packed with a prime selection of every likely lad in Taita and

Naenae. The place erupted into a giant brawl as one would expect. We eventually got the upper hand and locked up probably 100 plus for being in an unlawful gaming house. When I entered the hall one of my childhood associates took exception to me being there and threw a full half gallon of beer at me, missing me and smashing on the door lintel, drowning me in beer!! I had my good Court-going suit on and it was ruined. I took particular care to make sure I arrested him and no one else did.

A great time was had by all, offenders and cops alike. The guys were a bit browned off at being busted as they had all, as part of their admission fee, got a raffle – first prize a night with a woman of very easy virtue and very homely features who was set up at the back of the hall for business. I am not sure what second prize was but it may have been two nights with her!!

We transported everyone to the cells in Lower Hutt, processed them and then set up a then Magistrates Court in the Senior Sergeants office. In the meantime the lads had started a bonfire in the exercise yard so some of us had to get up on the roof with the fire hoses to put it out, half drowning them at the same time. After checks guys who were not wanted for anything else were bought before the beak in the special Court, fined $10 each way and released.

Years later, when working in late shift one evening in Whanganui I answered the counter. It was Barry Davis. He had come to ask if he could park his bus outside the station for security as he had bussed a party to Whanganui for a function of some sort. We had a great catch up and laugh about the last time we met. Barry passed a couple of years ago. He could be a mean dude but I knew a different Barry, a kid being brought up in a fatherless home prior to any DPB with several siblings, all poor as church mice and on struggle street and a Mum trying to cope alone. His father had been an American serviceman and abandoned the family when Barry was small. No excuse for his later misdeeds though.

Also Max has passed, RIP old friend. We used to call Max out at all times of the night and day when we were trying to interview Samoan guys who could not or would not talk English. Max had this unique interviewing style and we were always presented with perfect statements of admission. I also had the pleasure of working for a while in Central with Max's wife Constable Anna To'o. A lovely couple.

Cops, Cars and Wonderful Toys

Does anyone remember the Black Marias we used to use in the 70s and 80s? They were actually grey by then. Ever wondered where the term Black Maria or Black Mariah comes from?

From reading a tome about Police cars in the United Kingdom it appears the term is of American origin but was used in Britain and here.

An extract from The Amador Ledger- Dispatch dated 31 January 1902 states *"When New England was filled with emigrants from the mother country an African-American named Maria Lee kept a sailors' boarding house in Boston. She was a woman of great strength and helped the authorities keep the peace. Frequently the Police invoked her and the saying, "send off Black Maria" came to mean "Take him to jail". British seaman were often taken to the lockup by this woman and the stories the seamen spread of her achievements led to the name of Black Maria being given to the English prison van"*

Probably not a term that is used any more due to the PC brigade.

Have you ever wondered where the word cop comes from? I have. One theory I read recently is it is short for copper and arises from the use of copper police badges by the New York Police Department in the 19th century, making its way around the western world in the coming years. Another is it is French in origin.

One of the more interesting names for Police in NZ is John Hop from which the term "the johns" comes from. This seemed to be a term used by the generation born around the turn of the 20th century. I remember it being used by my grandparents. It may come from "John Hop the Cop" – who knows.

"Ds" or "D Men" was prevalent when I was a kid growing up in the Hutt Valley in the 1960s, referring to CIB staff.

Then we have the great English terms which are still used today in some contexts. "Peelers" from the founder of the modern English Police system Sir Robert Peel, "Busies", "Filth" – a term I have heard used in NZ as well in the 70s and 80s, "wooden tops" used mainly as a disparaging term for UB staff by the CID in the UK but also used here as well at times.

Then there is the Sweeney, short for Sweeney Todd, the cockney name for the Flying Squad from Scotland Yard. "Bluebottle" is a name, probably of UK origin, but heard in New Zealand at times.

A very old British term is "Beadle" to describe a law enforcement officer or church official. I have never seen or heard it used except in history books.

We then have the favourite of the Yanks in the 1970s – "The Fuzz" – no idea where or why this term came into being but we all used to joke about being picked up by the Fuzz.

The most common term after "cop" is of course "pig" – used commonly in NZ, Australia, the UK, the USA and Canada etc. Again – no idea of its origin but I did enjoy locking clowns up for calling me it in the 1970s before everyone got politically correct and the Courts decided that Police could not be offended by being called names or being sworn at. I do not remember any Judge actually asking me if I was offended or not.

As you would expect from Australia they seem to use the

words "rat" and "dog" for police as well as informants.

Who remembers when the police cars in New Zealand were black with a tiny red light above the windscreen? Growing up in the Hutt in the 1950s I used to watch these black beasts race around town. The most impressive was the 1955 Humber Super Snipe. They were big cars for their day and I do not remember them driving slowly. Rumour had it that the engine was a Commer truck engine but I will leave it to the car experts to comment on that. The Police in the Hutt also used the Ford Mark 1 Consul, a four cylinder version of the Zephyr and Zodiac models. I remember watching two cops trying to get a stroppy customer into the back of one at the Naenae shops when I was a little guy. The cops and the client were big blokes and the car just seemed too small for them all.

In the fifties the Police also used Wolseley 6/90s with the gear shift on the right hand side of the driver's seat and Vauxhall Victors for enquiry work. I am sure there were other models but, again I leave that to the expert historians to mention.

Of course the cops also had the Holden in the late fifties. We still had one or two at the Hutt station in the early 1970s, one being 676, the old prison van, by then painted grey and the other a CIB car. The Wharf Police in Wellington were still using a black PA Vauxhall Velox in the early 1970s. This had the "knee-cap remover" – the piece of windscreen surround that jutted out into the front door space.

We also had the "Flying Brick" – a grey van used by the fingerprint detectives to attend burglaries etc . It was a small Bedford van with sliding doors and the engine between the two occupants. It used to struggle up Ngauranga Gorge, not over-powered.

One of the best police cars I drove was the 1964 EH Holden.

We still had one or two at the Hutt in the early 1970s before the HQ Holdens arrived. These old buses could really motor and were very stable at cornering. The most unstable was the models following this model, the HD model. All cars at the time were manual with "three on the tree", drum brakes, no power steering and indifferent air conditioning. Automatics only began regularly appearing with the HQ series of Holden about 1973 onwards.

I believe that the Police came of age in terms of decent vehicles when the Holden Commodore was introduced about 1979. The Police also started returning sirens then, something that had been missing for about 15 years due to misuse by some scallywags. The Commodore was an Opel by another name and was a very nippy and roomy little car. We then changed to Fords which were great in country areas as they could go just about anywhere.

I would have liked to have driven the Snipe on patrol. It must have been challenging to navigate the back lanes and alleys behind shops in a beast that size.

In the early 1970s when we were using the 202 cu in, 3.3 litre 6 cylinder Holden HQ The Ministry Of Transport had V8 versions of the same vehicle which could actually catch errant motorists. The Police administration did not seem interested in offering powerful vehicles to us for some reason. The MOT always had the best cars, one of the best being the Mitsubishi V3000. It could really tramp and left our cars standing in any chase. At that stage we were using mainly Ford Falcons but Holdens were coming back into vogue again after an absence of some years.

The cars we used were all rugged and could take a lot of punishment. They were great fun to drive and being young cops we did have a lot of fun in them, usually without anyone seeing. Seat belts were installed in the cars but were usually wrapped around the handcuff bar behind the front seat until wearing them became compulsory in the early 1970s.

When I look at the Police nowadays and all the wonderful toys they have, the taser, the vest, the trendy baton, the weird looking cuffs and the comfortable uniforms I think back to the day I joined in 1970. We were still wearing the old dark blue serge or barathea uniforms with plastic shirts that had no pocket buttons. Every time you put on a clean shirt you had to fasten a set of buttons via ring clips to the shirt pockets. You could not iron the shirts, they would melt and whilst a light blue, they had a tendency to turn a bit green after a while.

The Police gave us two helmets, a white one for day and a navy blue one for night, females a silly little cap which served no real purpose. At least the helmets kept a bit of rain off. They were hopeless in the wind or when one needed to chase someone or wrestle with someone.

In those days we still walked a lot of beat and the only cops who had flat hats were Senior Sergeants or above and the Regulation 24 Constable serving as drivers. When one wanted a flat hat one had to apply for it and success depended on the state of liver of the Sergeant or Senior Sergeant getting the application. If he (very very few female NCOS in those days) did not like you no hat. If you were lucky enough to be put on an 'I' car for a shift you had to borrow a hat from a mate. In those days we were required to wear headgear when driving. Hopeless with the helmets due to the roof height of the Holdens we drove.

The navy-blue uniform was as hot as Hades in Summer. We were allowed to remove our tunics after 1 October each year, but had to start wearing them again from 1 April the following year. The dates may be a bit wrong but you get the gist. This was regardless of weather conditions or where one was serving in New Zealand. The department did provide a pair of shoes from memory but these were not really suitable for beat work so most of us bought our own boots, no reimbursement of course.

Getting back to the helmets, they looked smart but harkened back to Victorian and colonial times. We used to fasten a piece of yellow crayon onto the bolt holding the knob of the helmet. In those days we had to attend all injury or fatal motor accidents and used the crayon to mark vehicles, bodies and other debris at crash scenes.

There are legends of the old beat cops carrying their sandwiches in the helmet whilst on the beat as they could not guarantee getting back to the station for their meal breaks. I never saw this but who knows.

The helmets were generally loved by the public as they knew where to find a cop in a crowd.

The really good piece of kit we got was the night duty great coat. This was wool and weighed a ton but kept one warm when having a wee kip while on the beat on night shift. It had huge pockets, suitable for carrying items such as fruit and eggs to throw at other beat cops when one was a bit bored in the wee hours when the only other people around were the milkos, bakers and paper guys. A lot of us cut these down after joining the CIB and continued using them when on Crime Car patrol on nights.

We were given a wooden baton with a leather thong which we carried in a pocket in our trousers, a pair of handcuffs made by the Lithgow Small Arms Factory in Australia, carried either in a cute little black pouch on our German Army style belts or in the baton pocket and normal pocket on the other side of our pants. During day duty we had to carry cuffs otherwise batons were compulsory on Swing or Night shifts.

We were also given a plastic torch which lasted about five

minutes before it broke. We then had to buy our own torches but the departent did supply the batteries.

When we were issued our uniforms we had to sew the shoulder flashes on the tunics and great coat and the domes on the summer epaulettes and shirts ourselves. I wondered why I had to take a sewing kit to Trentham, I soon found out.

Our wet weather gear consisted of a navy-blue heavy raincoat. There were also capes but these had been phased out of general issue before I joined. The coats were not that waterproof, certainly not enough to prevent moisture getting in on an 8 hour shift on the beat. After a couple of years these were withdrawn and we received little plastic numbers that were actually water-proof.

No utility belts in those days, we carried everything in our pockets, including a revolver if need be. There was a cute little brown holster available but it was a pain to get on so most of us just grabbed the gun and six rounds and shot through.

The Police have come a long way in terms of personal equipment thank goodness. The modernization started in 1979 following the Moerewa Riots where local Police were severely injured and lucky not to be killed in a fight with a visiting gang. The Department introduced the PR24 baton and holder, a very effective weapon in the hands of a person trained in its use. We then began using softball helmets and shields on Team Policing when required. There was strict guidelines about the use of this equipment but it was the start of what we see today.

These were, in hindsight, not the good old days but we knew no different.

Car Chases

As a young cop in the Hutt 50 odd years ago I was always up for a car chase. In those days they were very few and far between but when they happened everyone wanted to get involved. There would be a line of police cars chasing the culprit, all very dramatic and exciting. A bit like something out of an American movie.

The station would empty out and every car in the yard would be gone in a flash. It was all on!! The poor old watchhousekeeper and/or Senior Sergeant then had to monitor the chase by radio and try to co-ordinate patrols to intercept the crims.

The crims cars were mostly clapped out old American V8s or Zephyr Mk 3s, old Holdens etc. None of the souped up performance cars we hear about now which seem to be responsible for a lot of silly young people dying needlessly. It seems there is not a week goes by nowadays that a chase has ended very badly with the death of someone. What has changed? The cars are much more powerful, maybe the driving skills are not what they used to be, but there seems to be a belief amongst young people that they are immortal.
I was involved, like many police, in many chases over the years. None ended in death. Most ended up with the car breaking down or running out of petrol or the occupants fleeing on foot in an isolated area, to be later tracked down by area patrols and dogs. Why is it that so many drivers or passengers are now killed? The Police seem to have a very sensible chase policy, including the requirement to abandon chases but on occasions after abandoning a chase it is not uncommon for the fleeing driver to still crash and die.

I feel for the Police concerned as no one wants a death. But the media attacking the police for chasing these young people is not right. If a driver is asked to stop by the Police then if they refuse they are breaking the law. Also the Police have a responsibility to protect innocent lives. It is becoming a very tricky situation and I am glad that I do not have to make the decisions necessary to either continue the chase or to abort it.

I have heard people comment that the kids driving the cars seem to think it is like a movie or a computer game and simply do not understand what they are getting themselves and their passengers into.

I understand that Queensland has abandoned chases full stop. I would be interested in hearing how that policy is working out.

The problem with having a policy of abandoning chases is that young hare-brained drivers know this and will continue to drive very dangerously until the Police are forced to abandon the chase, thereby making the situation much worse with the likelihood of a fatal outcome very much on the cards.
What to do? Not sure.

Secondary and Perking

I am not sure if "secondary employment" is done now in the Police but, whilst it was against the Police Regulations of the time, it was more observed in the breach than obeyed. Part time work or "secondary" was a huge tradition when I joined the job in 1970. Just about every cop I knew below the rank of Senior Sergeant had at least one part time job.

I indulged as much as possible as a way to make extra money to buy our first home. In those days many Police lived in rental accommodation, including Police houses for most of their careers, some retiring without ever owning their own home. The only way out of this situation for many of us was to find extra work on days off or between shifts to be able to save enough money for a deposit on a house.

I worked in many roles, truck driver, builder's labourer, roofer, home appliance service man, milkman, railways labourer, tennis court builder, haymaking, the list was endless.

I worked on section with trade-qualified guys who still did their trade between Police duties, guys who did security or bouncing work, guys who owned their own businesses with their wives. We were all very fit in those days and most of the secondary work was physical so it helped keep us fit for policing.

Now and again the boss would make an issue about secondary employment but I do not recall anyone being charged under the regulations. We just backed off for a week or two then carried on.

The only work I was not up for was security work or bar

work. This was too dangerous in terms of being seen and too much like my day job.

When I was stationed in Masterton secondary was rife. Just about everyone did it. A lot of farm work to be had. One summer in about 1974 half a dozen of us had just got a haymaking contract which was going to be very lucrative, but very hard work in those days before mechanisation. We were doing our first job between Carterton and Greytown, carting hay on the main highway from one farm to another to be stored in a shed when the Area Commander, Inspector Jim Waugh, out on his station inspection visits, saw three of us lined up in the back of the truck with another three in the cab, driving back to the paddock. He just about drove off the road!! We carried on expecting him to follow us but he did not thankfully.

The following day a station order appeared advising that anyone caught undertaking secondary employment without the permission of the Commissioner would be charged. Nothing more was said but we had to forgo our contract. Bugger!! I had plans for the money I was going to make.

A few weeks later we had a pay parade and one of the three Uniform Branch Sergeants at the station was absent, the boss noticing and asking why.. In those days attendance at a pay parade was compulsory unless you were on night shift, annual leave or in Court. Before anyone could reply someone called from the back of the parade that the Sergeant was tied up shearing and would not be able to make the parade. The boss had another blue fit and another Station Order came out the next day. The Sergeant had fairly red ears after he had been to see the boss. Nothing changed though, we just worked further out of town.

Some days I would knock off night shift, have two or three hours sleep and then get up and drive a general carting truck for the rest of the day, knocking off at 5 and going back to bed for another few hours kip. I shared the driving with another young Constable on another section and a Sinn Fein motorcycle gang member so the trucking company had the truck on the road every day. It was really hard work but very good money.

It was always enjoyable as we worked with good guys who had their own businesses and liked employing cops as they were honest, fit, reliable and normally intelligent enough to pick up skills quickly.

In those days, along with secondary there were perks. Perking is described in the Cambridge dictionary as *"an advantage or something extra, such as money or goods, that you are given because of your job". The term perking arises from "pecuniary advantage".*

When I joined Taylor's dry-cleaning would dry-clean our uniforms for free. This was fine, everybody used them but we all paid for our personal dry-cleaning. All good until one idiot started taking his family's clothing in to be dry-cleaned, demanding that the staff do it for free as he was a cop. The manager rang the boss to complain about the cop's attitude and that was that. No more free dry-cleaning.

Walking the beat was, for me, trips between cups of coffee or tea, usually at the Hutt taxi office or at a mate's car yard or shop. We also used to call for tea or coffee at Casualty when on Incident patrol at the Hutt, Masterton or Wellington Hospitals on night shift. The nurses enjoyed us calling as these places can be a bit rambunctious at time and having a couple of uniforms around helped. Calling at these places also resulted in us picking up a lot of info about various shady critters. Whilst we did not solicit refreshments we never said no when they were offered, except for alcohol of course. I have subsequently been told by more enlightened cops that this was "soft corruption". Hmmmm!!

When I started in Whanganui in the early 80s the early shift used to get free sausages from a local butcher for breakfast at 0600 hrs. This was a very longstanding tradition that was not abused until one cop arrived from another district. He was the ace "perker". One day on his day off he got up early, put his uniform on and visited the butcher shop before the patrol, picking up the sausages and returned home for a decent feed. The patrol crew turned up as usual to be told by the butcher that so and so had just called and picked up the sausages!! This put a stop to that perk!! The cop also then had to explain his actions to his colleagues.

McDonalds opened in Whanganui in the mid 80s and wanted to offer discounted meals to cops. The then District Commander stopped the practice forthwith. The manager of McDonalds wanted to encourage cops to come into his restaurant as it helped keep the peace. Oh well. I don't like Maccas anyway.

I would venture to say that "secondary" and "perking" are now not part of the Police culture. The perking was abused by some individuals, as seen above, but not by the vast majority. None of us thought we were doing wrong. Having contact with these people gave them security and companionship, usually at night, and also resulted in police finding out a lot about what was going in in their communities.

The Wages of Sin

In early 1975 I found myself at the newly-named NZ Police College in Trentham on my CIB induction course. I only knew one other guy there, Ross Pinkham. Pinky and I had gone through the Police cadets together. I was then stationed in Masterton and was a bit over-awed by all these big city cops who seemed so confident and clever.

We were met by the Course Co-ordinators Detective Senior Sergeant Bryan Hartley and Detective Sergeant Rex Miller who quickly explained the rules for the next 4 weeks. We were there to work and to work bloody hard. Our pass mark for daily and weekly tests was 80%. Exams were 60%. Failure in any will result in going home and back to section forever. I was a bit worried as this was the second such course run by the college. On the first one a few months before about a third of the course had failed. The instructors then said that we would not only be assessed on our academic results but also on bearing, social skills, the ability to get on with others etc. We were on trial in all facets of our lives for four weeks, if we made it that far.

The instructors told us that we were expected to study every evening but that we also had to attend the bar and take part in socialising with each other as well. I thought that this could be alright, I considered myself as a bit of a socialiser in those days.

I then had a worrying thought. I had not budgeted for the big spending required for serious socialising. My wife Jenny and I had just bought a section in Carterton and were paying it off, using all our disposable money, including secondary earnings so money was a bit tight. After the first night I had managed to get rid of my first week's social budget in about two rounds. I really wanted to pass this course so I needed a plan.

I noticed a few characters on the course had got together and started a poker school. Jim Mansell, Joe Townsley and Jim Ryan being three of them. Mmmm!! One of the benefits of growing up in my large extended Irish family was learning everything there is to know about horse racing and playing cards. I literally learned this at my grandmother's knee. My uncles all owned racehorses, some of which were quite successful, other family members were bookies.

The Old Man was an avid gambler and punter, everybody punted all the time. The family also played cards at every opportunity. I learned the basics of poker and blackjack as a wee tacker, taught by my grandmother using matches. In my teens in Naenae a couple of mates and I used to regularly attend a poker school run by an older brother of one of my mates. This guy was a serious dude and committed gambler but he let us play on occasions and taught us all a lot about poker. At some stage I moved on to healthier activities but I never forgot those lessons.

I decided to call in to the room where the little poker school was being run in Hut 235 and watched for a couple of nights. On the third night I asked timidly if I could sit in. Joe and the Jims welcomed me with open arms, easy sucker here. I quietly got my $1.50 change out and put it on the table. I spent a few rounds just sitting and watching, folding. Then after a while I had a few timid bets, making a little money. When I had about $5.00 on the table I discreetly removed the original $1.50 so that I was now only playing with my winnings. You have to be careful about doing this in some poker schools as it is against the protocols but these guys were alright. By doing this it showed that I never had much money at any one time. When I had about $10 of which there was about $4 on the table I quietly made my excuses about having to go back to study. In those days $10 could buy a lot of beer. I was alright for the week. I did the same once a week on all four weeks but different days and was able to pay my way in the bar, thus obtaining the assessment of being a bloody good guy to have a beer with by the two instructors.

Some reading this will know the rules but I will let a few go here. Never ever gamble if you cannot lose your stake. Never have a high profile in a poker game. Try never to make eye contact with others but watch them and their habits quietly. I did not know these guys that well and let them think I was a quiet kid from "over the hill" so they did not pay me much attention. This got a bit harder as the course went on as we all became friends and these guys were many things but stupid they were not. Never win too often but when you do play it down. Always bear in mind you are being watched as well. Never ever be the leader. All simple stuff but good training for life and doing deals or negotiating.

Many years later when I was a Senior Sergeant in Whanganui Jimmy Mansell was my Area Commander as an Inspector. Jim was a great cop and a bloody good guy. He loved fast cars all his life and was a real character. One day we were in his office shooting the breeze rather than talking about police matters we were dealing with at the time and I thanked him. He asked what for, I replied that he helped to subsidise my social costs at the induction course in 1975. He called me a cunning bastard but said he was happy to help.

Everybody on my induction course passed, the rest is history. Inspector Jim Mansell, Detective Senior Sergeant Joe Townsley, Detective Sergeant Jim Ryan – RIP my old friends.

Team Policing

In about mid 1973 I was sent with 140 other Constables, Sergeants and Senior Sergeants to Papakura Army Camp as part of the New Zealand Police Task Force. The course was to train us in crowd control and mass arrest procedures. It was all very physical and noisy. I do not remember much about the course other than we had no special gear except for great heavy green riot shields which probably came from the Army. We learned to do penetrating lines, flying wedges and offensive lines but all with short batons and normal helmets.

We all then returned to districts expecting big things but nothing happened. The big centres used their guys as part of their Team Policing Units, Auckland calling its unit the Task Force for some reason. Us other chaps, sorry no chapettes on the course, carried on doing our normal jobs and nothing really was ever said again about the National Task Force.

The years roll by. Team Policing Units become an established part of policing, especially in the main centres, and at some stage the Auckland Task Force became Team Policing as well. It all changed in August 1979 at Moerewa in Northland. A Stormtrooper gang from Auckland arrived in town looking for a dust up with the local Black Power gang who was nowhere to be found. The Stormtroopers wrecked the Okaihu pub and then went on the rampage. Local Police attending were attacked with weapons and missiles, police cars were burnt and Senior Sergeant Charles O'Hara, already injured, was thrown by gang members into a burning Police van. He was saved by other cops present at great risk to their lives. Police fired .38 pistols as warning shots but to no avail. One gang member was shot in the leg by the Police.

The local Police were outnumbered and all were severely beaten and badly injured. It was only the timely arrival of reinforcements from Whangarei that ended the riot. About 20 Stormtroopers were arrested.

This riot shocked the nation and caused a re-think of tactics by the top brass.

It seemed like overnight we had the PR24 baton, riot helmets, well softball helmets really, and decent shields. All staff were trained in the use of the long baton and it became part of our daily lives, carried, usually only at night and when needed, on our hips. This was a stark reminder to the public that the Police had changed. Prior to this we carried a short wooden baton in a long pocket on the side of our trousers, out of sight of the public.

We also all attended riot training, the same moves taught 6 years before in Auckland. Most districts and division stations formed their own part time Team Policing Units. The training was of a national standard so that Sections from different districts could meld together into Squads as required.

Our station boss in Lower Hutt, Chief Inspector Paul Wiseman, wanted a unit on the road every week to hit the Valley pubs and the taverns in Wainuiomata as required. A lot of these drinking outlets were pretty wild in those days with scraps most nights. The old Swing Shift week on the 5 week roster was the week each section worked as a Team Policing Unit on the Thursday, Friday and Saturday nights with a training day on the Wednesday. A van and two cars would be kept busy as a unit each night. Usually a Sergeant and up to 10 Constables with a dog as needed. Great fun. We tended to keep the cells full and the poor old watchhousekeeper flat out most weeks. On the odd occasion we would also have to call the Wellington Team Policing Unit for back up as well. Quite often we had call to use the helmets and on occasions, the shields, especially at private parties that had gone wrong. The shields were brilliant at stopping the odd bottle hitting one on the bonce.

The Springbok Tour rolls around and the days of the Red Squad and Blue Squad arrived. These specialist units did a marvellous job but the tactics they used were no different than that taught to us in 1973 with some modifications as needed.

As most cops in New Zealand had had basic Team policing training by the time the tour arrived most districts were able to field small Team Policing Units as required as well. There was the White Squad, the Purple Squad, the Tartan Squad, the Lower Hutt Mounted Foot etc. etc. All a bit of a light-heartedness really in a very serious situation. There was even one group of wallies who used green filing tape on their epaulettes, the Green Tape Squad. It kept us all laughing when there was not a lot to laugh about at times.

In 1984 we all trained up again in anticipation of an All Black tour to South Africa scheduled for 1985. Court action thankfully stopped this tour. Most districts by then had highly trained Team Policing sections who could easily form into Squads and Groups if needed to deal with public unrest.

I guess the terms Task Force or Team Policing are not Politically Correct now but the concept sure worked as a reactive response to very violent times.

Prisoner Escorts

Back in the day when life was in black and white and people walked and talked funny it was the responsibility of the Police in New Zealand to provide escorts for sentenced prisoners and large amounts of cash. I came into this near the end of this era but still got to do more than my share of both sorts of escorts as a young proby cop in the early 1970s. It was always the junior cop on the early shift who got stuck with driving around town with an old wages clerk, a great big .38 pistol in the pocket of the old baggy Police pants and a boot full of cash on pension day or some such other boring event. It got me off the beat for an hour which was good. A lot of guys did not even load the revolver, they just put the bullets in a pocket. The attitude was if there was a robbery let the dough go, who cares.

Prisoner escorting was another whole kettle of fish. It was made plain to us that our jobs were on the line if we actually lost a prisoner. Prisoners did escape but I never remember a cop losing his or her job over it unless they really stuffed up.

Escorts always seemed to be on a rostered day off for some reason, seriously interfering with a chap's secondary employment arrangements. We would be summonsed to the Senior Sergeant's office in smart plain clothes, given a warrant authorizing us to deliver little Johnny to the Superintendent of a named penal institution, a travel warrant for the prisoner and cop and a demand not to leave the prison without a signed "body receipt" from the Receiving Officer. The princely sum of $1.90 per 24 hours was paid as an allowance for this effort, nowhere as much as a chap could earn on his or her secondary job.

The most gruelling escort was to the Invercargill Borstal from anywhere in the North Island. The reason this institution was put in Invercargill can only have been to piss off the Police escorts from the North Island. At about the time I joined cops and prisoners were still taking the overnight ferry from Wellington to Lyttleton and then the South Island Limited from Christchurch to Invercargill. The cop then had to do the same in reverse after delivering the prisoner. It took days. No one flew back then as flying was still considered a luxury, especially for mere cops and smelly prisoners.

I never shared the joy of this experience, thankfully, taking a prisoner from Masterton to Borstal when flying was accepted as the most cost effective travel in about 1974. I did, however, do several escorts from Wellington to Waikeria, near Te Awamutu on the old Wellington to Auckland overnight Express. There was a "Correction Centre" at Waikeria Prison then where first time sentenced teen-age male prisoners were sent for a three month dose of discipline. For many this was the last time they went to prison as it was not a pleasant experience to undertake.

It was a bit of a trek so it was good if the prisoner was resigned to his sentence. If not it could get interesting. I always had a chat with my prisoner before we left, telling him we would buy food at Taihape and again maybe at Taumaranui if he was hungry and that he could have what he liked if he behaved. No booze though. We took handcuffs with us but I never had to use mine. The railway guards were also not keen on us handcuffing the prisoners to the seats for safety reasons.

These guys were young chaps, usually the first time away from home and more tearaways than serious criminals although some did graduate to serious crime later. We would take them to the toilet and leave the door ajar, explaining the need for this to them before we left. The toilets on the trains had windows which could be opened easily.

On one escort I met up with an old cadet mate, Garry

Blinkhorne, in Wellington Central and we were given three prisoners to take on the train to Waikeria. Garry was a real character and soon had the boys all on side with promises of food and smokes on the train. The boys were all resigned to their little holiday. We all travelled second class on the train and sat with other passengers in the carriage. On this trip there were quite a few young ladies sitting together in one area of the carriage and a guy with a guitar in another part of the carriage. It soon became clear that one of our boys was an accomplished guitar player and singer. They asked if they could have a sing-song. Garry and I could see no real reason to disagree so we all spent the evening sitting together singing and chatting with all the young ladies and the young guitar owner who was also very talented.

Neither the guys nor Garry and I let on that we were prisoners and cops. The girls must have just thought Garry and I were the only two who could afford nice clothes. One of us with one prisoner would get off at the stations with dining rooms and buy heaps of pies and cups of teas for the team. All good harmless fun.

About 4.00 a.m. we pulled into Te Awamutu railway station, woke our now sleeping charges and got off the train, saying goodbye to the ladies as one does, to be met by the night shift cop at Te Awamutu with the little grey Holden prison van. The boys and their belongings were put in the back and us in the front. Garry and I were pretty knackered by then as we had to stay awake of course.

The cop raced us around to the Commercial Hotel and woke the night porter who gave us a room to sleep in for a few hours. We were due to catch the Express at about 7.00 p.m. that night, so we had all day to kill in Te Awamutu. He then took the lads out to the prison, bringing back the body receipts for us.

Garry was also a bit of a charmer and he managed to bludge us a decent cooked breakfast after chatting up one of the housemaids. At about 10.00 a.m., breakfasted, we emerged onto the street in our reefer jackets and casual trousers. It was mid summer and hot as hades, no air conditioning in those days. We had all day to kill and the bar did not open until 11.00 a.m.

We decided to purchase some suitable clothing, t-shirts, shorts and jandals each. Suitably attired we then retired to the public bar of the Commercial at about 11.00 a.m. We remained there for the day playing pool against the locals, having a few quiet ones, not letting on we were cops and winning a lot of pool. We had to throw quite a few games as we did not want to piss off the locals and get turfed out.

At about 6.00 p.m. the late shift cop turned up in the same old van and took us back to the railway station for the trip back to Welly. By then we were full of fun and wanted to play. Guess what. There was another bunch of young ladies in our carriage on the way home. The old charmer Blinkhorne soon had us ensconced with these delightful companions singing and generally with the intent on having a good time all the way home until we both fell asleep after about ten minutes out of Te Awamutu, waking in the early hours of the morning and feeling a bit dusty!!   What boring company we were.

Dedicated to my Percy B Allen Cadet Wing mate Constable Garry Nicholas Blinkhorne - RIP old friend – one of the best.

Ninja Turtles - Memories

Most young people who take up policing have played some form of sport and seem to like a bit of rough and tumble so to speak. Policing will always provide the opportunity for this unfortunately. Sometimes our clients just did not like us or want to be with us so we would have to get all sweaty and maybe a bit shouty with them, even providing some hurty bits at times.

Over the years serving Police have always been involved in Boxing, Wrestling and the Martial Arts either as participants, coaches, referees or trainers.

Back in the 1970s Lee Jung Nam, 9th Dan Hapkido; 9th Dan Taekwondo, a very gentle but able Korean, bought his version of Hapkido to Wellington from his home country. This form of martial art became very popular with a lot of Wellington coppers at the time. Mr Lee used to run training sessions in the old Holland House gym from memory and a few different groups of Police would train with him over the years..

Hapkido only dates from the 1950s and is a medley of different martial art styles with self defence the priority.

Mr Lee had the support of the Police administration and he was much respected by all.

As a young guy I flirted with Boxing and Judo, enjoying the confidence and fitness these sports gave me. In 1975 myself and a CIB colleague and old school mate Pat O'Sullivan decided we would like to try a spot of Karate. The Hapkido sessions had not yet started in Wellington. We heard of the Petone Karate Club run by Rod Devlin, a 3rd Dan Karate Sensei (Master). We also heard it offered full contact free-style Suonji Ryu Karate training. This sounded a bit like us so we fronted up one night at the Sea Cadet Rooms on the Petone Esplanade where the dojo (training area) was.

There were about two dozen guys there, no females and no kids. We thought that this was interesting. However after our first training session we realised why. Whilst the club was open to females and children it was not the style of Karate most may have enjoyed. There was another cop there, Bill Dunn, later an Inspector in Wellington. I knew Bill was a top athlete in his day and a tough bastard. At the end of the formal training session Rod said that at this point newcomers were welcome to stay or go but that they were about to start Kumite or one-on-one sparring. Pat and I decided to give it a go in our footie gear, no fancy Karate suit at that stage. After about twenty minutes of being kicked, punched and thrown around the room we were then allowed to go (limp) home. I was sore for about a week but could not wait to get back into it. O'Sullivan also wanted more. We were up for a bit of pain.

Over the weeks we were joined by several other coppers, Terry Prisk, Terry O'Neill, and Bob Renshaw being three enthusiastic and very able members I remember. I even managed to drag my old mate Roger Bush along for a couple of sessions, a very capable exponent of the deadly arts.

Rod did not believe that a Black Belt should be awarded for at least five years after regular training begins. The grading system in the club was therefore very slow. It took Pat and I about four years to get to the stage of considering the Brown Belt grading, the last before Shodan (Black Belt). The club never indulged in breaking bricks or anything so pussy as that. It was a straight fighting club. As a result we did not compete against many other clubs except for the Victoria University Kyokoshinkai Karate Club and the Porirua Kempo Club run by Vern Winitana and his really tough crew. Both were free-style clubs and both had female members who were absolutely deadly.

The only parts of the body not to be hit in sparring sessions were the groin and head. This was observed in the breach quite often in the heat of battle. We wore boxes but no faceguards in those days, no gloves either. Injuries were frequent but one just got on with it.

As grading gets more senior there was a requirement to increase the number of fights or rounds for each grading so the three clubs would unite for grading sessions in order for there to be a sufficient number of Karateka (students) to spar or fight with. The Shodan (Black Belt) was traditionally 100 fights for an individual to survive, not necessarily win of course. The student would need to fight others from white belt (beginners) to black belt and back again in a grading session. The grade was immaterial when deciding fighting ability in these clubs as all grades tended to have tough scrappers in them, the more senior merely having more style. Fitness was a priority.

As would be expected our club attracted a lot of wannabes but they usually never stayed after the first sparring session, too hard and hurty. The most understated and shy individuals were the ones who see
med to be the most able at the end of the day.

The cops in the club were always singled out for a bit of treatment on interclub visits, as would be expected. We gave as good as we got.

The other, more important, side of Karate was the need to learn the moves, perform Kata (form). This is choreographed movement using various Karate techniques and brings about the spiritual side of the sport. It can be performed with or without weapons such as nunchakus. There was a strong emphasis on being humble both in the club and in normal life. Rod would never condone club members becoming involved in unnecessary fracas or violence away from the club. It would spell the end of the membership for anyone who did that.

The club later moved to Upper Hutt where we were joined by Bob Bopp, a then Traffic Officer, later a serving Police officer. Bob is a very capable Karateka and a good guy.

Rod needed to move on due to work issues so the club folded in the late 70s as there was no other respected and competent Sensei able to carry on.

I enjoyed my time in Karate. I dabbled with other styles but missed the all-out mayhem I was used to in Sounji Ryu Karate. Any fighting discipline or style gives an individual quiet confidence in other areas of life. One learns how to push oneself very hard to achieve objectives if one has trained hard in sport. I never did get the Black Belt but that's ok. Jenny says I am a Black Belt in other ways.

Surveillance

Ex-CIB staff will remember the surveillance exercises from their Induction or Detective courses, having to track a subject through the streets of Wellington on a busy Friday night without being snapped.

I was hopeless at mobile surveillance. I saw the absurdity in the whole exercise which did not help my approach to what is a recognised policing skill. When we were told that our Induction course would be trailing a couple of young coppers through the streets on a busy Friday shopping night in Central Wellington in the mid 1970s I thought it was a waste of time. Firstly the young cops will be looking for us, secondly we were not allowed to dress casually, we all had short hair and the males were wearing two or three piece lounge suits. Anyway we did the exercise and most were snapped within a very short time. I know it was about training in the different moves and tactics but I could not get into the game.

About a year later I was on Indecency Squad under the tutelage of two excellent Detective Sergeants, Ted Lines and Bryan Toomey. We were all sitting at our desks writing off dodgy stair dancing files, doing arrest files, listening to Ray Whitham explain the intricacies of arson investigation or playing the old office joke on the Captain, Detective Senior Sergeant Colin Lines, one fine morning.

The Captain had a glass fronted office looking out over his realm of three squads, Indecency, Robbery and one other squad whose name escapes my now, maybe Shopbreaks. Also in the mix were the three pillage boys, Billy Humphries, Blip Holmes and John Wimsett. About 20 staff. The Captain liked to saunter out to the main office in his way, being the big cheese. If the phone rang in his office he would race back in to answer it, might be Detective Chief Inspector Wally Baker or Police National Headquarters. The boys watched him and when he wasn't looking one of us would ring his extension. He would race back into his office and just as he got to the phone we would hang up. This would go off and on all day. I never found out if the Captain ever twigged but maybe not as John Kelly did very well in the CIB.

Anyway, I digress.

Rangi Rangihika, the boss of the drug Squad, calls in from his lofty office on the third floor, deigning us with his august and highly secretive presence. He met with the Captain in the glass-fronted office with the door shut.

The Captain then calls Ted, his brother, into the office. Two more different brothers it would be hard to find. More secretive talk.

Ted comes out of the office, gets us Indecency team into the interview room with Rangi and The Captain and we are briefed on a surveillance exercise, a real one. Early the following morning, a busy week day, we were to tail a suspected drug dealer from his home near Williams Street in Petone to the Petone railway station, about two miles, on foot. We were to accompany him on the train without him knowing we were there and then follow him when he got to town. No worries, sounded like fun and there could be a free breakfast thrown in. One of us asked if we could wear jeans etc. The answer from the Captain was "No you will wear your normal suits". Someone suggested we might stand out but no, suits it was to be.

Now, in those days Petone was very much a working class town with huge industry and anybody walking the suburban streets in a suit was either a Detective or a Mormon. Plus we all not only had suits on but we looked like what we were, cops. Short hair, tallish, not pretty boys, well-built and with that weird way of walking that cops have. Now I know crims are said to be stupid but

I have met some bloody clever crims in my time. Most involved in serious crime are of at least average intelligence otherwise they would not survive at that level for long in the underworld. They are also really paranoid about cops.

As I was standing alone on the Cuba Street overbridge freezing my whatsits off, waiting to take over from Paul O'Shea when he and the subject emerged onto Cuba Street I thought how ridiculous this was. People driving to work were beeping me, some giving me the fingers, some waving, old mates from school wondering why poor old Ratts is standing all alone on top of a bridge in a suit and tie at about 7.30 a.m. on a freezing winter's morning.

Paul comes into sight with chummy and his girlfriend in front of him. Paul is particularly fetching in his blue checked two piece flare-bottomed suit with his platform shoes on. Chummy is dressed in the normal working clothes for the area, P jacket, beanie and jeans. I start following him in my two piece green suit and platform shoes, not quite as fetching as O'Shea on this day. I follow the subject for about half a mile when Heather Staines took over. She at least fitted in a bit better, being smartly dressed in a casual way. We all caught the train at Petone and ended up in Welly, the guy was picked up by the Drug Squad and tailed somewhere and we all were told "off you fuck, back to work". End of story.

The guy knew he was being followed as he crossed the street two or three times on me alone. Never knew what happened to him, being a lowly Detective Constable it was probably above my paygrade.

Years later we ran an operation in Whanganui to catch some dealers. The Surveillance team came up from Wellington to help us. Now I know they were very dedicated and that they took their roles very seriously but Whanganui is not Wellington. It is a quiet little

238

provincial town. The team arrive in their souped up little Jap cars, all looking very serious and earnest, all in long hair and casually dressed, all white. We had a brilliant Neighbourhood Watch set up in Whanganui with dear old folk ringing us all the time about suspicious vehicles and people. It was hard work being a daylight house-breaker in Whanganui in the 80s. The team went out to do its thing. We all bemusedly got on with our inquiries. Next thing the section staff is racing out the station, burglars on in Whanganui East, 10.30 in the morning!! They catch the culprit, a white guy in a raced up Jap car sitting in Pepper Block, a very poor part of town, predominately brown and very quiet with a great Neighbourhood Watch co-ordinator. After a couple of similar incidents it was decided that maybe we did not fit the criteria for mobile surveillance.

Now I don't know about you but even as an ex-cop I still retain some paranoia about who is hanging around my neighbourhood. I eyeball any guy sitting in a car outside my house or near-by, waving out to them or, on some occasions, taking their number plate.

Do we think crims are any different. They have more to lose than coppers do.

The worm Turns

Being a cop has never been easy. The Police are open to criticism, debate and hate all the time. They are subject to the opinions of arm chair warriors who have probably never ventured onto a sporting field or at least had a decent front to front stoush in their lives. Society is full of self-appointed experts on policing and people who just basically hate the police no matter what their socio-economic situation is, the more educated the more virulent sometimes.

Back in the olden days, Christmas 1975 to be exact, I was a young Detective Constable on duty over the Christmas period with the rest of my crew, the Car Squad. It was a wonderfully warm Christmas and all the boys had their walk shorts on with the long socks and the biro tucked into the top of the socks. We also had our ties on, full Windsor knots of course, no letting the team down sartorially.

Early on Christmas Day morning we were all at our desks trying to get Supreme (High) Court files ready for trial, writing off enquiries, preparing arrest files, all the stuff of hard working detectives everywhere, hoping for a quiet day of correspondence then home early to our families. Not to be!!

One of the crew, acting as CIB receptionist, came into the squad room saying Mr so-and-so, a well- known, high profile, cop-hating septic sod, was in the office with his young teenage daughter. They had come into the station to report her being raped by two strangers in Kelburn on Christmas Eve.

Mr So-and-so was quite muted and actually almost pleasant to deal with. His poor daughter was deeply shocked and distraught. She was taken under the tender care of our only female detective on the squad, Dianne Berry, and our Detective Sergeant, Pat Moore.

The late then Detective Kevin Kalff, the late Hilary O'Donnell and myself were assigned the scene, a bungalow on the side of a hill in Kelburn. The victim reported walking home down the street when two Pakeha males grabbed her, dragged her into the house and raped her repeatedly for some hours before she was allowed to go. The victim was a teenager from a very good home, very sheltered and very intelligent. She was able to provide a sound good description of both offenders via Identi-Kit pictures.

One offender had distinctive looks.

Meanwhile Kalffy got his little team organised and we attended the scene, no one home. The door was open so we began the scene examination anyway. The house was, as I said, on the side of a hill but with a large area enclosed underneath, not a basement as such but just the area of foundation.

We spent most of the day at the scene and left a scene guard after we finished. Somehow a noise was heard from under the floor area. The staff on the scene began to search this area, probably something we should have done when we got there, and found our two suspects hiding.

Both were taken back to the station for a chat. They initially denied any involvement but found it very hard to explain the reason for hiding all day while the Police were tramping around their flat above. From memory they both agreed to individual ID parades and were both picked by the victim. Both then made statements admitting their sins and subsequently received lengthy prison terms.

Why I remember this particular crime nowadays is the attitude of the father towards the Police after we had locked the offenders up. He was in tears and his gratitude was overwhelming

This guy was a serious dude when it came to making our lives miserable via the courts and newspapers. He turned that day, once he realised that the only people in the world who could help his dearly loved daughter were the people he had, for many years, hated and despised so much. We were suitably embarrassed and abashed but I think we all learned something about human nature that day, all young coppers starting in our careers.

Dedicated to Inspector Kevin Kalff and Detective Constable Hilary O'Donnell, both great cops and terrific mates. RIP.

Why Do People Become Cops

What is it about being or having been a cop that binds many ex Police together as we age? A very few spent or will spend their whole working life in blue. The rest of us did our time, no matter what that was, and move on to other careers, jobs, businesses and professions. Most do very well in their lives after Police but very few forget their time in the job.

Was it the training and teamship provided at the police college or the shared experiences of watching each other's backs, dealing with death, working very close together in highly charged and very dangerous situations and depending so much on each other? Is it the demographic and personality types we all seem to come from, the similarities that are looked for by the recruiters when we all first walk into the local station to apply. Most cops and ex-cops seem to get on well and respect each other. A few never fit in and move on.

Is it due to the fact that probably most of us played sport as young people, champions or not, and learned how to "get on" with each other and other teams or players? That most of us are (or were) physically strong and able?

Was it the values our parents or caregivers instilled into us as children?

Were we all born with a mission wired into us to want to help and protect others from evil when most other people are afraid to? When there is a facebook group in this small country with over 6000 ex and serving NZ police as members and another group just for ex police of 800 and growing there has to be something in the water, don't you think?

I know ex-military do the same thing so there may be the commonality, memories borne from the trauma of bad things happening whether it is the sheer horror of war or the frightening and cumulative incidents that Police have to attend. Do Firies and Ambos have such a site or continue to associate after their sterling service to their communities?

I was a cop for the first half of my working life, 23 years. I then spent 21 years working for ACC in injury rehabilitation, most of that time working with the most disabled and severely injured clients and their families.

I worked with great, talented, very well-educated colleagues, great people each and every one, with the exception of the odd knob, but we get those everywhere. ACC was a brilliant employer. However I do not hark back to those memories much at all, other than to wonder how some client I was close to is faring. I still go back to the police stories and the guys and gals who I enjoyed working with all those years ago.

Is it because as we age things seem to be better in the past than they really were? Personally I believe things were better, especially for police. Society has changed so much now I suspect that whilst policing as an art will never change, only develop and improve with technology, the job is a lot harder than when I left in 1992.

For me this has lead to an interest in our Police history, which I find fascinating, hence me sharing stories from long ago. What my research shows me is that the craft of policing stays the same, society changes and methods change but the nuts and bolts of working with victims and offenders, the communication skills and basic investigative techniques needed have not changed in many years. Any changes are driven by technology, the law and society, nothing that the average copper has any real control over.

Police Values – Comment to Serving and Ex-Police

I think I am getting a bit grumpy as well as old. Maybe I should stop reading the Police Association magazine. Every few months there is a letter from someone talking about values, leadership etc. like these are new components of policing. I once read an article from a serving Police Officer about Values and Culture which was quite a good article overall and he or she is dead on the button about what is expected from leaders but he/she ruined the whole argument when he/she said the following –

"We can't expect people to take directives from the executive about culture change seriously when they appear to demonstrate the worst behaviours of the old culture that we are trying to move away from, or condone that behavior through silence and inaction."

What is this "old culture" that was obviously around when most of us older folk wore blue? From what I can gather from this and other observations there is a story being propagated out there nowadays that we were actually quite bad people and I do not know how to correct this.

Yes we had a few bad bosses, as I am sure the modern Police have now. Yes we had a few bad cops as I am sure exist today but they were dealt with as needed. It seems that now Police verge on sainthood. When I talk to present serving Police I often hear the term "back in the day" referring to some practice or rather that is no longer done or countenanced.

The Police have a long and proud history in this country but there seems to be a drive from those who train our new cops to demonise past police as racist, misogynist, corrupt, sexist, violent and all the other names that are now popular to describe a male-dominated culture of the past. I guess we did have members who could be described as above; as I am sure the Police have today also. They were very much in the minority and tended to be sorted eventually.

What has changed to make the current Police think they are so perfect? I know society has changed but criminals are now worse than ever, much more dangerous than when I was a cop. Crime still needs hard-nosed policing as criminals are actually very bad people, not victims as some would have us believe. They choose an outlaw lifestyle because they like it. The country needs Police that can deal with that if needed.

The anecdotes I hear from older serving Police worry me a lot. I have heard that a young cop, when asked to attend a sudden death, declined, saying he did not sign up for that. What happened then? A Sergeant at a concert was detailing staff for duties. Two female cops told him they would only work with each other as they went through the college together and just ignored his instructions to work with others. What happened then?

These are anecdotes and so I do not guarantee their veracity at all but there must be some basis for them. In my day these members probably would not have acted like this anyway but if they did they would have been told in no uncertain terms who wore the stripes in this discussion. Apparently that has changed. I do not blame the cops for this behaviour, I blame the training and "culture" that allowed them to think like this. Like most serving and ex-police I was very proud of having been a cop and it really upsets me to think that the current Police administration is educating new staff to believe that we were not as true-blue as we actually were. I worked with the best people this country could produce but I also worked with a very few ratbags who were let go as soon as their behaviours were uncovered, many gaoled. Why do the Police go to the default setting of these terrible examples of Police when judging me and my ex-colleagues?

Finally

From the above you will see that the New Zealand police had its origins in both a national paramilitary police model based on the Royal Irish Constabulary and a provincial civil policing model based on the Metropolitan Police in London. As the frontier society that New Zealand was in the mid-19th century slowly became settled and the New Zealand Wars stumbled to an end around 1872 there was no real need for a standing armed force ready to go to war at a moment's notice, but otherwise acting as a coercive police.

The Armed Constabulary began to be disestablished by St John Branigan, ending in the mid-1870s, after his death and the New Zealand Constabulary force made up of ex Armed Constabulary personnel and the personnel from the provincial forces was formed as a stop-gap measure. There were still occasional flare-ups between Maori and European well into the 20th century so coercive force or staff trained in such tactics was still required for some time.

From about 1877 to 1886 the New Zealand Constabulary Force slowly looked forward to becoming a total civil and, partly, unarmed police based purely on the model portrayed by the Metropolitan Police.

With the formation of the New Zealand Police Force in 1886 police who had served in either provincial police services or the Armed Constabulary, or both, transferred into the new police. As you may have read, this was not without its problems. Many police were semi-literate and basically trained soldiers unable or unwilling to adapt to a civilian policing lifestyle. Personal behavior and moral standards of many police were mostly that expected of soldiers, not police officers. As a result many were let go and new members entered the new police but still via the military training of the Permanent Artillery until the end of the 19th century.

All very novel and it took many years and a few Royal Commissions of Enquiry to establish a police service worthy of the name. Of course, New Zealand was still transforming as well from the frontier society of tough European pioneers and hardy Maori fighters, a male-dominated society where drinking, fighting and gambling were the norm for most single and many married working men.
T
he development of the police in New Zealand has been a mirror of the development of New Zealand as a civil society. The police really did not enter the 20th century in many ways until the mid-1950s following yet another Royal Commission. The result of this commission and the subsequent guidance of Samuel Barnett, assisted by the largesse of the government purse provided by then Prime Minister and Minister of Police Sydney Holland, is the New Zealand Police we have today. A modern, forward-thinking, diverse and increasingly well-educated service with modern equipment and technology.

Even this service took many years to finally develop as a modern police service that can foot it with any western police service anywhere in the world.

Despite being an outwardly unarmed service since 1886 police have always carried or had ready access to weapons. New Zealand has always been a heavily-armed society so the ability to deal with armed criminals has ever been a priority for police. The stories above show a butchers bill of dead police sadly, especially for a period in the 1950s and early 1960s. Policing is a dangerous career because of the nature of those being policed.

When researching for this book I was saddened to realise just how violent and hard the lives of early police were. Not only did they have to deal with very dangerous criminals but their own working conditions, pay and equipment was abysmal until well into the 1950s. The command structure was rigid and autocratic, harking back to the military-based policing of the late 19th century. The promotion system was archaic, based on filling dead men's shoes. Any Constable with ambition had at least 14 years to wait for promotion to Sergeant. No wonder turnover of staff was a constant issue.

Even as an ex police officer I have learnt a lot while writing this book. I am grateful that my career in the police was during more enlightened times. Those old boys had it tough back in the day.

If you have got this far I hope you enjoyed most or all of the stories.

Bibliography

Bainbridge, Scott, *Shot in the Dark: Unsolved New Zealand Murders,* Allen & Unwin 2010

Butterworth, Susan, *The History of Policing in New Zealand, Volume 5, More Than Law and Order – Policing a Changing Society 1945 – 92,* University of Otago Press, 2005

Carr, Margaret, *Policing in the Mountain Shadow*, TNL Print, 1989

Derby, Mark, *The Prophet and the Policeman – The Story of Rua Kenana and John Cullen*, Craig Potton Publishing, 2009

Dunstall, Graeme, *The History of Policing in New Zealand, Volume 4, A Policeman's Paradise, Policing a Stable Society – 1918 to 1945,* The Dunmore Press

Green, David, *Martin Cash, Te Ara Encyclopaedia of New Zealand,* 1990.

Hill, Richard S, *The History of Policing in New Zealand, Volume 1, Policing the Colonial Frontier 1767 to 1867*, VR Ward, Government Printer, 1986

Hill, Richard S, *The History of Policing in New Zealand, Volume 2, The Colonial Frontier Tamed; New Zealand Policing in Transition, 1867-1886,* GP Books, Historical Branch, Department of Internal Affairs, 1989

Hill, Richard S, The *History of Policing in New Zealand, Volume 3, The Iron Hand in the Velvet Glove, The Modernisation of Policing in New Zealand 1886-1917*, The Dunmore Press, 1995

Joseph, George, *By a Person or Persons Unknown – Unsolved Murders in New Zealand*, The Law Book Company Limited Sydney, Melbourne, Brisbane Perth, 1982

McGill, David, *No Right to Strike – The History of the New Zealand Police Service Organisations,* Silver Owl Press, 1992
O'Hara, C. R., *Northland Made To Order, A District Police History*, Books of Oceania, 2005

Singe, Michael & Thomson, David, *Authority to Protect – A Story of Policing in Otago*, Tablet Printing Company, Dunedin, 1992

Walker, Trevor, *Slain On Duty – An Account of New Zealand Police and Traffic Officers Killed On Duty 1886 to 1996* - Print Communications Limited, Wellington, 1996

Walters, Brian, *A history of the Waikato Police*, Brian Walters and the Waikato Times, Hamilton, 1986

Ward, Alex S, *Memories of Constable A.S Ward*, Times Commercial Printers, Hamilton, 1991

Young, Sherwood, *Guilty on the Gallows, Famous Capital Crimes of New Zealand*, Grantham House, 1998

Young, Sherwood, edited by, *With Confidence and Pride – Policing the Wellington region 1840 – 1992,* Wellington Police Trust, 1994
Police Ten One Magazine – April 2018
Truth Newspaper 8th September 1923

Young, Sherwood, edited by, *With Confidence and Pride – Policing the Wellington region 1840 – 1992,* Wellington Police Trust, 1994
Police Ten One Magazine – April 2018
Truth Newspaper 8th September 1923